Eric Voegelin *circa* 1945. From a painting by Conrad Albrizzio
Photograph by William Mills

Autobiographical
Reflections

Autobiographical Reflections

ERIC VOEGELIN

EDITED, WITH AN INTRODUCTION, BY

ELLIS SANDOZ

LOUISIANA STATE UNIVERSITY PRESS

BATON ROUGE AND LONDON

Copyright © 1989
by Louisiana State University Press
All rights reserved
Manufactured in the United States of America

First Printing
98 97 96 95 94 93 92 91 90 89   1 2 3 4 5

Designer: Albert Crochet
Typeface: Linotron Trump
Typesetter: The Composing Room of Michigan, Inc.
Printer and Binder: Thomson-Shore, Inc.

Library of Congress Cataloging-in-Publication Data

Voegelin, Eric, 1901–85
   Autobiographical reflections / Eric Voegelin; edited, with an
introduction, by Ellis Sandoz.
      p.   cm.
   ISBN 0–8071–1515–0 (alk. paper)
   1. Voegelin, Eric, 1901–85. 2. Philosophers—Germany—Biography.
I. Sandoz, Ellis, 1931–   . II. Title.
B3354.V884A3 1989
193—dc20
[B]   89-32051
                                                              CIP

In consideratione creaturarum non est vana et peritura curiositas exercenda; sed gradus ad immortalia et semper manentia faciendus.

In the study of creature one should not exercise a vain and perishing curiosity, but ascend toward what is immortal and everlasting.

St. Augustine, De Vera Religione

Contents

Contents

Introduction

Eric Voegelin's *Autobiographical Reflections* allow Voegelin himself to survey and interpret in brief compass the vast work of his lifetime down to 1973 when the *Reflections* were dictated and transcribed. They provide the best possible introduction to the person and thought of a man who was a remarkable scholar and arguably the greatest philosopher of our time. Here Voegelin explains Voegelin, in an autobiographical account calculated to elucidate his other writings and set them in the overall horizon of his thought. Authoritative, incisive, elegant, and profound as they are, the *Reflections* both disclose the motivations of Voegelin's remarkable scholarly work in various stages of development from the 1920s onward and also reveal at least something of the affable, witty, courageous, tenacious, tough, deeply principled, and learned human behind the work familiar to those who knew him well. Publication of the *Autobiographical Reflections* of Eric Voegelin is a major intellectual event.

An elaborate introduction to a book this brief and accessible would be out of place. But a few words summarizing the facts of Voegelin's life and the origins of the *Reflections* as a document will perhaps be pertinent and helpful to the reader.

Erich Hermann Wilhelm Voegelin was born in Cologne, Germany, on January 3, 1901, and died in Stanford, California, on January 19, 1985. He was the son of Otto Stefan and Elisabeth Ruehl Voegelin, and his father was a civil engineer. The Voegelins lived in Cologne and in Königswinter in the Rhineland until 1910, when they moved to Vienna, where Eric attended school and the University of Vienna, ultimately becoming an associate professor of political science there in the Faculty of Law. He was promptly fired by the Nazis after the Anschluss in 1938 because of his opposition to Hitler (given expression especially in four books published between 1933 and 1938), and he narrowly escaped arrest by the Gestapo as he fled to Switzerland. Shortly thereafter, he emigrated with his wife (the former Lissy Onken, whom he married on July 30, 1932) to the United States. After a year tutoring in the government department at Harvard and commuting during the second semester to teach at Bennington College in Vermont, Voegelin taught summer school at Northwestern in Evanston, Illinois. The Voegelins then took a short vacation in Wisconsin before moving to the University of Alabama in the fall of 1939, where they remained for two and one-half years.

In January, 1942, Voegelin joined the faculty of the Department of Government of Louisiana State University. He remained in Baton Rouge until January, 1958, and was selected one of the first three Boyd Professors at LSU, writing and publishing during sixteen years in Louisiana the books in English that made his reputation: *The New Science of Politics* (Chicago, 1952), from the Walgreen Lectures of the previous year; and the first three volumes of *Order and History*: volume one, *Israel and Revelation*; volume two, *The World of the Polis*; and volume three, *Plato and Aristotle* (LSU, 1956, 1957). He and Lissy became American citizens in 1944 and retained their citizenship thereafter. Voegelin accepted an appointment in 1958, however, as professor of political science at the Ludwig-Maximilian University in Munich, establishing the new Institute for Political Science there. During this period, the principal publication was *Anamnesis* (Piper, 1966), which directly presented the philosophy of consciousness underlying the work in English. After a decade, the Voegelins returned permanently to the United States in 1969. For a five-year period ending in 1974, Voegelin held an appointment at Stanford University as Henry Salvatori Distinguished Scholar in the Hoover Institution on War, Revolution, and Peace. It was during this time that the present *Autobiographical Reflections* were produced. At the end of the period, the fourth volume of *Order and History* finally was published—after a seventeen-year hiatus—entitled *The Ecumenic Age* (LSU, 1974.) The Voegelins continued to live in Stanford after retirement, where

Eric is buried, and where his wife survives him. They have no children.

In addition to the books mentioned, some one hundred articles and essays were published during Professor Voegelin's lifetime; and voluminous materials were left unpublished in manuscript, including much of a four-thousand-page study entitled "The History of Political Ideas": parts of this work were absorbed into *Order and History*, and eleven chapters were drawn together, edited by John H. Hallowell, and published under the title *From Enlightenment to Revolution* (Duke, 1975). Some eight volumes comprising "The History of Political Ideas" are planned for publication in the *Collected Works*. The fifth volume of *Order and History* was published posthumously under the title *In Search of Order* (LSU, 1987), as the capstone of Voegelin's revolutionary philosophy of politics, history, and consciousness.

That and in what sense Voegelin's work may be understood to be revolutionary is argued in my *The Voegelinian Revolution: A Biographical Introduction* (LSU, 1981), and the *raison d'être* of the *Autobiographical Reflections* lies in work done in preparing that study. For Voegelin in 1973 was far from concerned with writing an autobiography or a memoir—beyond what he already had done with the anamnestic experiments conducted in 1943 but only published in 1966 in *Anamnesis*. These fascinating sketches of recollections covered experiences from his boyhood that he found formative for his consciousness as a human being, beginning at fourteen months with his very first recollection and coming down to about age ten. In 1972 and 1973, he was hard at work completing *The Ecumenic Age*, which came out a year later. My own work required greater detail about his biography than was readily available, so I began conducting tape-recorded interviews on subjects of importance to my study of his thought. These ranged over many subjects, and matters finally came to a head during the summer of 1973 while I was visiting Stanford for the purpose of gathering information and began trying to put together a chronological and thematic account of Voegelin's intellectual development. After several false starts, we hit on the procedure of holding a series of interviews, conducted on the basis of my queries, which would be responded to in an oral narrative dictated by Voegelin. To be sure the transcription could be made accurately, his secretary was present to take down everything in shorthand. All of this was done in the few days between June 26 and July 7 (we celebrated July 4, of course), in Voegelin's study at his residence on Sonoma Terrace—amidst clouds of cigar smoke from the eighteen or so King Edward cigars he consumed each day, the fierce and frequent barking of the two pet Pekinese dogs that, despite Mrs. Voegelin's best efforts to keep them quiet, repulsed dangers on every side, the hum and clatter of the lawn mower, roar of the vacuum cleaner, and frequent jangle of the telephone. (These atmospherics have been purged from the text, but since I have just listened to the twenty-seven hours of recordings again in preparing the manuscript for publication, they are vivid in my memory as I write and were most definitely part of the "experience" fifteen years ago.) The transcription then was read and corrected by Voegelin and retyped in due course to form the revised document that I subsequently named the *Autobiographical Memoir* of Eric Voegelin and quoted *in extenso* in my book. It is now retitled for independent publication.

What Eric Voegelin's autobiography might have looked like had he sat down purposely to write one on his own volition we cannot know. My inquiries elicited the responses we have here. The questions asked and answered were ones, apart from basic information of a factual kind, that seemed most pressing for a full and precise understanding of material I had studied by and with Voegelin since my undergraduate days in his theory survey at LSU in 1950. Whatever the complexities of the subject matter, Voegelin's great gift as a teacher was his capacity to expound it simply, lucidly, and tellingly in living speech. This talent I luckily turned to advantage in my interviews with him that became, in effect, a private seminar running for two or three hours each morning for nearly a fortnight. What began as a rather *pro forma* exercise that (I sensed) was conceived partly as a means of putting an end to persistent questioning and of getting rid of a questioner who was bidding to become a troublesome distraction from "the work," took on unexpected life. Voegelin warmed to the subject. He then proceeded to conduct, under prodding and somewhat unwillingly at first, then in resignation, and finally with a relish reserved for "the work" itself, what gradually turned into a further anamnestic search of the reality of Eric Voegelin whose story rises in its best moments into the meditative discourse of high philosophy. Even cold on the page, the result is a triumph in which all can rejoice.

A word about mechanics: after Section 11 the incisions and headings are mine; larger insertions by the editor are in brackets; minor emendations in syntax are made silently, as in copy-editing; words dropped from the text inadvertently but audible on the tape have been restored *when* they clarify meaning; any words italicized for emphasis are by the editor. Since the obvious provenance of this manuscript was that of a background working paper for a study written by someone else, Voegelin did not take the meticulous care in making emendations that he would have taken with a manuscript of his own that he would see through to final publication. With great caution, I have tried to fill this gap.

Autobiographical
Reflections

1

University of Vienna

I attended the University of Vienna, in the Faculty of Law, from 1919 to the completion of my doctorate in 1922. The atmosphere of the university at the time was determined by the breakdown of the Austro-Hungarian Empire at the end of the First World War. By its composition, the university was still the university of the capital of the Empire and reflected in its scholarship and the personal attitude of the professors this metropolitan atmosphere. At the time when I was a student, and throughout the 1920s, or rather until the effects of National Socialism made themselves felt in the early thirties, Vienna still had an enormous intellectual horizon and was leading in science internationally in a number of fields. First, there was Hans Kelsen's Theory of Pure Law, represented by Kelsen himself and the growing number of younger men whom he had educated, especially Alfred von Verdross and Adolf Merkl. Second, there was the Austrian School of Marginal Utility. Eugen Boehm-Bawberk had already died, but Leopold von Wieser was still the grand old man who gave the principal course in economic theory. Among the younger economists there was Ludwig von Mises, famous because of his development of money theory. Joseph A. Schumpeter was in Graz at the time, but his work of course was studied. Among the further intellectual and spiritual components that would impress themselves on a young man at the time was the school of theoretical physics going back to Ernst Mach, and represented at the time by Moritz Schlick. An important intellectual force in this circle was Ludwig Wittgenstein, less by his presence than by his work. There further must be mentioned the Austrian Institut für Geschichtsforschung, represented by Alfons Dopsch, who by that time had attained international fame through his work on the history of Carolingian economics.

Among the younger men, there was the rising force of Otto Brunner, who later became famous by [his theories of medieval feudalism, especially as published in *Land und Herrschaft* (4th ed., 1959)]. A further glory of the University of Vienna at the time was the history of art, represented by Max Dvořák and Josef Strzigowski. Dvořák had already died by the time I came to the University, but Strzigowski was active. I had courses with him in the history of Renaissance art; and what especially was attractive about him was his interest in Near Eastern art, of which his two-volume work about Armenia is a great document. At the same time there was flourishing in Vienna the Institut für Urgeschichte.

More on the fringe so far as I am concerned were such famous institutions as the Institute for Byzantine Music under Egon Wellesz, with whom I later got acquainted. After the National Socialist takeover, Egon Wellesz went to Oxford. A further inevitable massive influence was represented by the psychologists. I took courses under Hermann Swoboda, who was very much addicted to the theory of rhythms of Ernst Kries; and he, in turn, was a close friend of Sigmund Freud. Into the psychology of Swoboda entered as a background his early friendship with Otto Weininger. The works of Otto Weininger were read by everybody at the time. The most important influence in psychology, of course, was given through the presence of Freud. I did not belong to the circle of Freud and never met him, but I knew quite a few of the younger men who had been trained by him. The most important at the time whom I knew was Heinz Hartmann, who later came to New York; Robert Waelder, who later established himself in Philadelphia; and Kries, who later went to Australia.

Now about the composition of the Law School. The great intellectual figures by whom the students were attracted at the time were Hans Kelsen, the lawyer and maker of the Austrian constitution, and Othmar Spann, the economist and sociologist who had developed a theory of universalism and had carried out a structural analysis of a people's economy, going in its content far beyond the subject matter dealt with by the more restricted marginal utility theorists. The third figure who attracted students in masses was Carl Gruenberg, a stalwart of Social Democracy. In the wake of the upheaval through the breakup of the Empire and the establishment of the Republic in 1918 came the ascendancy of the Social Democratic party, and in the first election in which I ever participated I voted for it; an important figure had become the chief ideologist of the Social Democrats, Max Adler. More on the periphery, so far as I was concerned, were a number of excellent lawyers—for instance, Strisower in international law; Schey, who had conducted the reform of the civil code; and Hupka in civil procedure.

I had registered as a student for the curriculum that would lead to the *Doctor rerum politicarum.* My decision to take these courses leading to the doctorate in political science were partly economic, partly matters of principle. So far as economics are concerned, I was very poor, and a doctorate that would be finished in three years had a definite appeal. The law doctorate would have required four years. The matter of principle was a vague but strong impulse even at that time that I would embark on a career in science. The doctorate of law had the temptation that ultimately one could land, if one did not become an independent lawyer, in a civil service position; and I did not want to become a civil servant. The choice of political science was furthermore determined by the attraction of the faculty, which included such famous men as Kelsen and Spann. An alternative, seriously considered by my father, who was a civil engineer, and myself at the time, was to go into physics and mathematics. But politics had the stronger pull. Still, after I had finished the doctorate in political science, I enrolled in the Philosophical Faculty in mathematics courses, especially with Philipp Furtwaengler in *Funktionentheorie.*

But these studies turned out to be no more than desultory, because I simply could not become enthusiastic about mathematical problems.

During these three years I began to form personal relationships with students of my own age, some of them not more than one or two years older and, by virtue of that slight age difference, coming back from military service, which had given them a maturity that people such as I (who had escaped military service by my youth) found attractive. The occasions on which these relationships were formed were the courses we heard in common, and especially the seminars. Three of these seminars were of major importance for the later cohesion among the group of young men about which I have to talk. I mention first the seminar with Othmar Spann, not because it was the most important under this aspect but because here I got acquainted with some people who later dropped out of my life. The general climate of the Spann group and of the young people attracted by Spann was Romanticism and German Idealism with a strong touch of nationalism. Some of these people later got involved in National Socialism or in even more radical national movements opposed to National Socialism. At the time when the Hitler problem became virulent in Austria, contacts with these people faded and were not resumed later. Still, I have to mention this phase, because to Spann and the work in his seminar, especially his private seminar which I attended through several years, I owe my acquaintance with the Classic philosophers (Plato and Aristotle) and with the German idealistic systems of Johann Gottlieb Fichte, G. W. F. Hegel, and F. W. J. von Schelling. More important for my later life, apparently because it met with my own inclinations, were the seminars of Kelsen and Mises. Through the Kelsen seminar, and again especially the private seminar, were formed the connections with its older members, particularly Verdross in international law and Merkl in administrative law. Among the people closer to my own age group were Alfred Schütz, who later became professor of sociology at the New School for Social Research in New York; Emanuel Winternitz, who, after

4

we were all thrown out by Hitler, became the curator of the collection of musical instruments in the Metropolitan Museum of Art in New York; Felix Kaufmann, the legal philosopher who became professor at the New School for Social Research; and Fritz Schreier, who, when he came to America, entered the independent business of marketing and advertising. Third comes the private seminar of Ludwig von Mises, which I attended for many years, until the end of my stay in Austria, and where I formed connections with Friedrich August von Hayek, Oscar Morgenstern, Fritz Machlup, and Gottfried von Haberler.

From these groupings, determined by the institutions of the seminars and the personal friendships and relations between these people and others, there crystallized in the end an institution which, with ironical overtones, was called the *Geistkreis* [Spiritual *or* Intellectual Circle]. It was a group of younger people who met regularly every month, one of them giving a lecture on a subject of his choice and the others tearing him to pieces. Since it was a civilized community, it was a rule that the man in whose house we met would not be the one to deliver the lecture, because the lady of the house was permitted to attend (otherwise women were not admitted), and it would not be courteous to tear a gentleman to pieces in the presence of his wife. To this group, which gradually expanded with sometimes somebody dropping out, belonged on and off most of the people just enumerated, especially Alfred Schütz, Emanuel Winternitz, Haberler, Herbert Fuerth, Johannes Wilde the art historian, Robert Waelder the psychoanalyst, Felix Kaufmann, Friedrich von Engel-Janosi the historian, and Georg Schiff. An important characteristic of the group was that we were all held together by our intellectual interests in the pursuit of this or that science, but that at the same time a good number of the members were not simply attached to the university but were engaged in various business activities. A man like Alfred Schütz, for instance, was the secretary of a bankers' organization and later entered a banking business. He continued his banking activities when he came to New York and had the fantastic energy of pursuing both his business successfully and of becoming the author of the studies that now have become famous through his collected works. Emanuel Winternitz was a practicing lawyer connected especially with *Bausparkassen*. He used a good deal of his income as a successful lawyer to make extended trips to Italy in order to indulge his interest in art history. That was the basis on which he later established himself in America, leading ultimately to his position in the Metropolitan Museum of Art. His great success is the organization of that marvelous permanent exhibition of musical instruments that has attracted the attention of the visitors to the museum since 1972.

The economists were affected by the shrinking of the University of Vienna under the conditions of the Republic. One university could not accommodate as many first-rate economists as emerged in these years, and the names of Hayek, Haberler, Morgenstern, and Machlup have become famous in England and America. They intended to leave Vienna even before Hitler. Machlup was one of the last to leave, because he was an independent industrialist. Engel-Janosi, besides being an excellent historian, was the owner of a parquetry factory; but I must say that the successful conduct of his business was largely due to the eminent business intelligence of his wife, Carlette. A further difficulty arose through the fact that, beginning with the establishment of the Republic, anti-Semitism became an ineluctable factor in the University of Vienna. At the time I entered the university as a student, a considerable number of the full professors were Jews, reflecting the liberal policy of the monarchy. But after 1918 and establishment of the Republic, no more Jews were appointed full professors, so that the younger people who were Jews had no chance of ever rising beyond the level of *Privatdozent*. That limitation was in part responsible for the necessity of excellent men like Felix Kaufmann and Alfred Schütz to pursue their business occupations. Schütz, as I have mentioned, was a banker; Felix Kaufmann was a director of the Anglo-Persian Oil Corporation. Many of these young people, through the advent of Hitler, the fact of being thrown out of their positions, and the necessity to flee, were thrown into their business careers. The friendships formed in these years held up. The members of this *Geistkreis* were physically dispersed, but the personal relationships have remained intact.

2

High School

The development of my studies in the university requires some reflection on the background acquired in high school. I went to a *Real-Gymnasium*, which meant that I had eight years of Latin, six years of English, and as an optional subject, two years in Italian. Besides, my parents took care that I had some elementary tuition in French. The school was further characterized during the war years of 1914 to 1918 by the drafting of a number of the regular teachers for military service, so that certain courses were supplied by persons exempt from military service who came from outside the regular teaching personnel. These happened to be the most influential for us teenagers. Especially should be mentioned the English teacher Otto Erwin Kraus, who so far as I know had been a journalist in England before returning at the beginning of the war to Austria and entering the teaching service. He was a knowledgeable intellectual who was especially interested in psychoanalysis in the variety of Alfred Adler. One of the high points of my high school education was the study of *Hamlet*, during a semester, as interpreted by Alfred Adler's psychology of *Geltung*.

One of the regular teachers was Philip Freud, an excellent physicist and mathematician, who taught us so well that in the last year of high school (eighth grade), a friend of mine, Robert Maier, and I were quite able to become interested in the Theory of Relativity, which had just become famous; and Albert Einstein's presentation of his theory of 1917, which had just come out, is still one of my most valuable possessions. We studied it and at first could not understand it, but then we discovered that our difficulty was caused by the simplicity of the theory. We understood it perfectly well but could not believe that something so simple could arouse such a furor as a difficult new theory. The mathematical apparatus, of course, was entirely at our disposition. When we encountered these seeming difficulties of understanding, we consulted with Freud, our physics teacher, and found out about our problems and received further information.

I remember especially from such a session with Freud his bringing to our attention that, according to the new theory of atoms, when you take a saw and cut through a piece of wood, you separate atomic structures. How it is possible to separate atomic structures by a handsaw was for him the greatest puzzle in the structure of physical reality. Freud had seen the problem of reduction and the autonomy of the various strata in the reality of being.

The stratification of reality led to an incident in another connection. One of the very good people who came from the outside during these years was a chemist from the Polytechnik in Vienna, Strebinger. I was called up for an oral test after I had been absent from a lecture in which the question of the composition of citric acid had been discussed. I had learned the matter at home and knew all about citric acid, but I could not answer the question of how one obtains it, because I thought there was some complicated chemical process involved. Then I was thundered down as an egregious jackass, because I did not know that citric acid is obtained by squeezing lemons. I got a bad grade that semester.

Another man from the Polytechnik who was of importance was Kopatschek, the mathematician. In mathematics, after we reached the prescribed level of differential calculus, we went further with enthusiasm into the theory of matrices and some hints at group theory. This wide range of interest represented by very good teachers will explain my receptiveness when I came to the university. But before I came to the university, in the vacation between the *Abiturium* and the beginning of my university studies in the fall, I studied the *Kapital* of Marx, induced of course by the current interest in the Russian Revolution. Being a complete innocent in such matters, I was of course convinced by what I read, and I must say that from August, 1919, to about December of that year I was a Marxist. By Christmas the matter had worn off, because in the meanwhile I had attended courses in both economic theory and the history of economic theory and knew what was wrong with Marx. Marxism was never a problem for me after that.

3

Max Weber

This problem of throwing out an ideology because it is scientifically untenable remained a constant in these years. Very important for the formation of my attitude in science was my early acquaintance with the work of Max Weber, whose volumes on the *Sociology of Religion*, as well as *Wirtschaft und Gesellschaft*, came out in these years and were of course devoured by us students. The lasting influence of Max Weber can be concentrated in the following points. First, the essays of Max Weber on Marxism going back to 1904–1905 completed my rejection of Marxism as untenable in science, which had been prepared by the courses in economics and in the history of economic theory that I had taken earlier. Second, Weber's later lectures on *Wissenschaft und Politik* made it clear that ideologies are so-called "values" that have to be premised when one acts but are not themselves scientific propositions. The question became acute through Weber's distinction of *Gesinnungsethik* and *Verantwortungsethik*—ethics of intention and ethics of responsibility, as they are usually rendered in English. Weber was on the side of the ethics of responsibility— *i.e.*, of taking responsibility for the consequences of one's action, so that if one for instance establishes a government that expropriates the expropriators he is responsible for the misery that he causes for the people expropriated. No excuse for the evil consequences of moralistic action could be found in the morality or nobility of one's intentions. A moralistic end does not justify immorality of action.

This fundamental insight of Max Weber, even though he did

not analyze its implications fully, remained a firm possession. Ideologies are not science, and ideals are no substitute for ethics. As I later found out, the distinctions of Max Weber were closely connected with the neo-Kantian methodology of the historical sciences developed by the so-called Southwest German School of Rickert and Wilhelm Windelband. In Weber's context, it became clear that social science, if it wanted to be a science, had to be value-free. That meant for Weber that the sociologist had to explore relations of cause and effect in the social process. The *values* that he would use to select these materials were premises and not accessible to scientific treatment; value judgments thus had to be excluded from science. That left him with the difficulty that the premises of selection of materials for science, as well as the premises for an ethics of responsibility, had to remain in the shadow. Weber could not analyze these areas. The external symptom of this gap in his theory is the fact that in his sociology of religion, wide as it ranged, there was no treatment of early Christianity or of classic philosophy. That is to say, the analysis of experiences that would have supplied the criteria for existential order and responsible action remained outside his field of consideration. If Weber nevertheless did not derail into some sort of relativism or anarchism, that is because, even without the conduct of such analysis, he was a staunch ethical character and in fact (as the biography by his nephew, Eduard Baumgarten, has brought out) a mystic. So he knew what was right without knowing the reasons for it. But of course so far as science is concerned that is a very precarious position, because students after all want to know the reasons why they should conduct themselves in a certain manner; and when the reasons—that is, the rational order of existence—are excluded from consideration, emotions are liable to carry you away into all sorts of ideological and idealistic adventures in which the ends become more fascinating than the means. Here is the gap in Weber's work constituting the great problem with which I have dealt during the fifty years since I got acquainted with his ideas.

But, third, before going into that matter, I should stress that one important further influence of Max Weber was the range of his comparative knowledge. So far as I am concerned, Weber established once and for all that one cannot be a successful scholar in the field of social and political science unless one knows what one is talking about. And that means acquiring the comparative civilizational knowledge not only of modern civilization but also of medieval and ancient civilization, and not only of Western civilization but also of Near Eastern and Far Eastern civilizations. That also means keeping that knowledge up to date through contact with the specialist sciences in the various fields. Anybody who does not do that has no claim to call himself an empiricist and certainly is defective in his competence as a scholar in this field.

4

Comparative Knowledge

To continue the problem of comparative knowledge, Max Weber of course was not the first to set this example. The founder of sociology, Auguste Comte, also insisted on having this broad range of knowledge, and this range has remained ineluctable for the great social scientists ever since. The matter has been obscured by recent restrictive definitions of sociology, so that thinkers like Comte are today classified as philosophers of history or historical sociologists. Such classifications, however, do not abolish the structure of reality. The necessary empirical range of knowledge is still the basis of all serious science in these matters.

As a matter of fact, it was already clear in the early twenties, when I started into the field as a student, that comparative historical knowledge was a requirement. The model of Max Weber in this respect was fortified by Oswald Spengler's *Decline of the West*, a work that should not be considered only under the aspect of its dubious classification of civilizations and of the dubious organic analogies, but above all as the work of a man who acquired the historical knowledge that made possible the comparative study of civilizations. The background for Spengler's work was of course the great *History of Antiquity* by Eduard Meyer, whose work in the following decades was also the basis for the work of Arnold J. Toynbee. If one looks at Toynbee's text, especially that concerning ancient civilizations, one will find Meyer is the most frequently quoted authority.

It was my good luck when I was a student for a semester in

Berlin in 1922–23 to be able to take a course with Eduard Meyer in Greek history. He was a very impressive personality. He would walk in, a tall figure slightly stooped by age with a great shock of hair, step up to the lectern, fold his arms on it, close his eyes, and then talk for the full hour without interruption, in impeccable language, never making a grammatical or stylistic mistake and never getting tangled up in a sentence. When the bell sounded, he would conclude the lecture, open his eyes, and walk out. What was particularly impressive about Eduard Meyer was his treatment of historical situations from the point of view of the person engaged in the action. I still remember his masterful characterization of Themistocles on the eve of the Battle of Salamis, weighing the possibilities that could lead to victory. I like to believe that Meyer's technique of understanding a historical situation through the self-understanding of the persons involved has entered my own work as a permanent factor.

This range of knowledge represented by Eduard Meyer should be supplemented by the memory of a man of less weight in the critical detail, but of a similar range and comparative vision—Alfred Weber. I had the good fortune to spend a semester in Heidelberg in the year 1929, when he delivered his course in the sociology of culture for the first time. Again, it was brought home to me that a scholar, if he wants to talk about social structures in their historical context, must have comparative knowledge and be as much at home in the genesis of Babylonian civilization as in the genesis of Western civilization in the time of the Merovingians and Carolingians.

5

Stefan George and Karl Kraus

The range of knowledge for comparative purposes was more than a formal principle. As these various recollections indicate, I actually acquired a considerable amount of knowledge for such comparative purposes through the study of the works of Max Weber, later of Alfred Weber, Eduard Meyer, Spengler, and Toynbee. This acquisition of knowledge was very importantly favored in those years by the influence of the so-called *Stefan-George-Kreis*. Stefan George is today chiefly remembered as the great German poet in the period of Symbolism, and as such he undoubtedly also had an influence on me. Through him I became aware of Symbolist lyrics and began to study with some attention such French poets as Stéphane Mallarmé and later Paul Valéry.

The importance of George, however, at that time lay chiefly in his influence on a considerable number of his adherents and his immediate friends and pupils who became scholars in their own right and determined the climate of the German universities for the intellectually more alert younger generation. Of the men whose works I absorbed intensely at the time, and whose volumes in first editions are still part of my library, I mention Friedrich Gundolf, especially his *Goethe*, *History of Caesar's Fame*, and *Shakespeare und der Deutsche Geist*; as well as Max Kommerell's *Jean-Paul* and his volume on the German Classic and Romantic literature, *Der Dichter als Führer*; Ernst Bertram's *Nietzsche*; Wilhelm Stein's *Rafael*; and Ernst Kantorowicz's *Kaiser Friedrich II*. Then, of course, there is the work of the classical scholars belonging to the circle of Stefan George, extending over the twenties, beginning with the work of Heinrich Friedemann, who was killed in World War I, on Plato, which was continued by Paul Friedländer's and Kurt Hildebrandt's work on Plato that became fundamental for my own studies, which were continued in their spirit.

A further influence of the first magnitude began to develop rather early in the twenties, became very intense after my return from America and France in 1927, and lasted until the death of Karl Kraus in 1937. Kraus was the great publicist who published *Die Fackel* [The torch], which appeared at irregular intervals and, as well as his other literary work, was read by everybody among the younger people whom I knew. It was the intellectual and *moraliste* background that gave all of us a critical understanding of politics and especially of the function of the press in the disintegration of German and Austrian society, preparing the way for National Socialism. The fundamental position of Karl Kraus was that of the great artist of language who would defend the standards of language against its corruption in the current literature and especially through the journalists.

His work, like that of Stefan George, must be understood in the context of the fantastic destruction of the German language during the Imperial period of Germany after 1870. We have no precisely comparable phenomenon in England, France, or for that matter in America at the time. Regaining language was a matter of deliberate effort on the part of the younger generation. The influence of my schooling by the style of the *Stefan-George-Kreis* can still be discerned by anybody who cares to pay attention to such matters in my first books, in *Über die Form des amerikanischen Geistes* and especially in *Die Rassenidee in der Geistesgeschichte von Ray bis Carus*. Regaining language meant recovering the subject matter to be expressed by language, and that meant getting out of what today one would call the false consciousness of the petty bourgeois (including under this head Positivists and Marxists), whose literary representatives dominated the scene. Hence, this concern with language was part of the resistance against

ideologies, which destroy language inasmuch as the ideological thinker has lost contact with reality and develops symbols
for expressing not reality but his state of alienation from it. To
penetrate this phony language and restore reality through the
restoration of language was the work of Karl Kraus as much as
of Stefan George and his friends at the time.

Particularly influential in the work of Karl Kraus was his
great drama of the First World War, *Die Letzten Tage der
Menschheit*, with its superb sensitivity to the melody and vocabulary of phoniness in politics, war patriotism, denigration
of enemies, and ochlocratic name-calling. Kraus's critical
work, with its first climax in *Die Letzten Tage der Menschheit*,
was continued throughout the 1920s in his criticism of the
literary and journalistic language of the Weimar Republic in
Austria and Germany. It increased in importance with the gradual emergence of National Socialism to dominance on the public scene. The second of his great works dealing with the major
catastrophes of the twentieth century was his *Dritte Wal-
purgisnacht*, treating the phenomenon of Hitler and National
Socialism. A restrained version of this work was published in
the last year of his life in *Die Fackel*. The restraints were due to
his fear that the full exposition of the swinish catastrophe
could hurt people who were potential victims of the man in
power. The complete and unrestrained text of the *Dritte Wal-
purgisnacht* was published only after the war by the Kösel-
Verlag in Munich as Volume I of the *Werke*, which run into
sixteen volumes. I should say that a serious study of National
Socialism is impossible without recourse to the *Dritte Wal-
purgisnacht* and to the years of criticism in *Die Fackel*, because
here the intellectual morass that must be understood as the
background against which a Hitler could rise to power becomes visible.

The phenomenon of Hitler is not exhausted by his person.
His success must be understood in the context of an intellectually or morally ruined society in which personalities who
otherwise would be grotesque, marginal figures can come to
public power because they superbly represent the people who
admire them. This internal destruction of a society was not

finished with the Allied victory over the German armies in World War II but still goes on. I should say that the contemporary destruction of German intellectual life, and especially the destruction of the universities, is the aftermath of the destruction that brought Hitler to power and of the destruction worked under his regime. There is yet no end in sight so far as the disintegration of society is concerned, and consequences that may surprise are possible. The study of this period by Karl Kraus, and especially his astute analysis of the dirty detail (that part of it that Hannah Arendt has called the "banality of evil"), is still of the greatest importance because the parallel phenomena are to be found in our Western society, though fortunately not yet with the destructive effect that led to the German catastrophe.

6

The Pure Theory of Law: Neo-Kantian Methodology

I shall now go into the question of my more immediate studies as a student in the university and my veering toward Kelsen's Pure Theory of Law. I cannot say with precision why Hans Kelsen was for me a more strongly attractive teacher than Othmar Spann. Spann's range was without a doubt much larger, both philosophically and historically, than the range of Kelsen's work. What attracted me, so far as I recollect, was the precision of analytical work that is peculiar to a great lawyer. The success of the Pure Theory of Law, and its continuing importance in the philosophy of law, lets one sometimes forget that Kelsen was a practical lawyer who drafted the Austrian constitution of 1920 and became a member of the Verfassungsgerichtshof. His commentary on the constitution he drafted shows his juridical acumen to its greatest advantage. What I learned from Kelsen, I should say, is the conscientious and responsible analysis of texts as it was practiced in his own multivolume work and in the discussions in his seminar. His work was inseparable, of course, from the Pure Theory of Law itself, which furnished a logical analysis of a legal system. This analysis of the system, culminating in Kelsen's conception of the *Grundnorm* (basic norm), still stands today. It has been improved in numerous details, as for instance by Merkl's elaboration of the *Delegationszusammenhang* as well as by the expansion of the system by Verdross beyond the constitutional *Grundnorm* to the fundamental norm of international law. There have been further refinements through the studies of the younger men like Felix Kaufmann, Fritz Schreier, and Emanuel Winternitz, but on the whole Kelsen's analysis was complete and could be improved only in this or that detail. This fact explains why there has been no great further development of the Pure Theory of Law. It was the splendid achievement of a brilliant analyst, and it was so good that it hardly could be improved upon. What Kelsen did in this respect still stands as the core of any analytical theory of law. I later used this core, with some improvements of my own, in the courses in jurisprudence that I gave in the School of Law at LSU. I should like to stress that there never has been a difference of opinion between Kelsen and myself regarding the fundamental validity of the Pure Theory of Law.

My differences with Kelsen's theory began to evolve gradually. That I was not a simple adherent can be gathered from the fact that I made my own Ph.D. with both Spann and Kelsen as doctor-fathers, a feat greatly admired by the younger people at the time because the universalism of Spann and the neo-Kantianism of Kelsen were considered to be incompatible. The differences evolved from ideological components in the Pure Theory of Law, which are superimposed on the logic of the legal system proper but do not affect its validity. They can be removed while leaving the core of the theory intact. This superimposed ideology was the neo-Kantian methodology, which determined the field of a science by the method used in its exploration—in this case, by the logic of the legal system. Since in the conventional terminology of the time the field that Kelsen represented as a professor was *Staatslehre* (political theory), and since neo-Kantian methodology circumscribed by its method the logic of the legal system, *Staatslehre* had to become *Rechtslehre* (theory of law), and everything that went beyond *Rechtslehre* could then no longer be a part of *Staatslehre*. That, of course, was an untenable position. At the time, I did not have a full understanding of the rather primitive semantic games involved in such misconstructions, but at least I sensed them. It was obviously impossible to deal with the problems of the *Staat*, and of politics in general, while omitting everything except the logic of legal norms. Hence, my difference from Kelsen developed through my interest in the materials of a political science that had been excluded from *Staatslehre* understood as *Rechtslehre*. In 1924 I published my first essay, of rather dubious scientific quality, entitled "Reine Rechtslehre und Staatslehre," in which I confronted the *reine Rechtslehre* with the materials dealt with by German *Staatslehre* of the early nineteenth century. Already at that time I conceived the task of the future political scientist to be that of reconstructing the full range of political science after its restriction to the core of the *Normlogik*.

That requires a few remarks about the problems of neo-Kantianism as it presented itself to me as a student in the 1920s. There were several neo-Kantian schools. The one that was dominant in the person of Kelsen was the so-called *Marburger Schule* of Hermann Cohen. Cohen, in his interpretation of Kant's *Critique of Pure Reason*, concentrated on the constitution of science by the categories of time, space, and substance—*science* meaning Newtonian physics as understood by Kant. This pattern of constituting a science through the categories applied to a body of materials was the model for the construction of the Pure Theory of Law. Everything that would not fit into the categories of *Normlogik* could no longer be considered science. There were, however, other neo-Kantian schools, above all the so-called Southwest German School represented by Windelband and Rickert, who dealt with the constitution of the subject matter of historical sciences by "values." That branch of methodology goes back to the 1870s, when Albrecht Ritschl, the Protestant theologian, distinguished for the first time between *Tatsachenwissenschaften* (sciences of facts) and *Wertwissenschaften* (sciences of values). The terms chosen betray the origin of the problem in the early dominance of the natural sciences as the model of science. Against their prestige, poor fellows like theologians, historians, and incipient social scientists had to establish that their fields were sciences, after all, too.

That is how "values" were invented. In Rickert's conception, values were certain cultural forces about whose reality nobody could have any reasonable doubt, such as state, art, and religion; the materials selected and related to these values would be the subject matter of the science of art, religion, and the state. This technique of reconstituting the historical and social sciences by the so-called *wertbeziehende Methode* (*i.e.*, by reference to a value) suffered from the grave defect that values are highly complex symbols, dependent for their meaning on the established "culture" of Western liberal society. It was very well to assume the *Staat* to be a value that determined the selection of materials, but this selection would run into all sorts of difficulties because the model of the *Staat* was the Western nation-state, and it would be difficult to bring the Greek *polis* under this head and still more difficult to bring an Egyptian empire under it. Moreover, values had to be accepted. And what did one do if somebody did not accept them, like for instance certain ideologists who wanted to establish a science by relating materials not to the value of the state but to the value of its withering away? The apocalyptic, metastatic dreams of, for instance, Marxist ideology, going back to Fichte's Johannine conception of the withering away of the state, simply did not fit into the constitution of a political science under the value of the "state."

7

Political Stimuli

When I became aware of such problems, I had not yet even an inkling of their magnitude. I shall turn now to the gradual enlargement of the horizon that permitted me to discern their nature.

The stimuli for going deeper into the matter were provided by political events. Obviously, when you live in a time dominated by the recent Communist revolution in Russia, Marxism (and behind Marxism the work of Marx) becomes a matter of some importance for a political scientist. I began to get interested in the problem of ideologies. The second great stimulus was, of course, provided by the rise of Fascism and National Socialism. I studied the movements as they developed, and in one instance, the National Socialist case, I went into the questions of biological theory that were implied in the National Socialist race conception. My two books *Rasse und Staat* and *Die Rassenidee in der Geistesgeschichte*, both published in 1933, are the result of my preoccupation with biological theory. This interest in biology, as well as a certain amount of technical knowledge about genetics, went back to my studies in 1924–25 in New York, when a number of my friends were young biologists like Kurt Stern, who worked on drosophyla genetics in the laboratory of Thomas Hunt Morgan at Columbia University. The numerous evenings spent in the company of these young people, my frequent visits to the laboratory, and the familiarity I acquired with the development of mutations were an invaluable basis for understanding the problems of biology involved in the race question. The result of my studies, of course, was not quite compatible with National Socialism, and the second one of the books mentioned, *Die Rassenidee in der Geistesgeschichte*, which presented the genesis of the idea from its beginnings in the eighteenth century, was withdrawn from circulation by the publisher and the remainder of the edition was destroyed. That is the reason why this book, which I consider one of my better efforts, has remained practically unknown, though it would be of considerable help in the contemporary, rather dilettantic, debates between evolutionists and anti-evolutionists. Biological theory has remained one of my permanent interests, just as physics has so remained from my initial start on its problems in my last years of high school.

A further broad range of materials that had hitherto escaped my notice was again imposed by a political stimulus. After 1933 Austrian resistance to National Socialism led to the civil war situation of 1934 and to the establishment of the so-called authoritarian state. Since the conception of the authoritarian constitution was closely related to the ideas of the *Quadragesimo anno*, as well as of earlier papal encyclicals on social questions, I had to go into these materials; and I could not get very deeply into them without acquiring some understanding of their background in Thomistic philosophy. In the years 1933–36, my interests in neo-Thomism began to develop. I read the works of A. D. Sertillanges, Jacques Maritain, Étienne Gilson, and then got even more fascinated by the not so Thomistic but rather Augustinian Jesuits like Hans Urs von Balthasar and Henri de Lubac. To this study, extending over many years, I owe my knowledge of medieval philosophy and its problems.

8

Concerning My Dissertation

Its subject matter was *Wechselwirkung und Gezweiung. Wechselwirkung* was the key term of Georg Simmel's sociology, which formed the basis for the further development of the *Beziehungslehre* in German social science. *Gezweiung* was the favorite term in the sociology of Othmar Spann. The difference was the ontological one of constructing social reality out of relations between autonomous individuals or of assuming a preexistent spiritual bond between human beings that would be realized in their personal relations. My concern was with the difference between Simmel's individualistic and Spann's universalistic construction of society. The dissertation was never published, and I am afraid I hardly remember now the details.

9

Concerning Oxford in 1921 or 1922

I was lucky enough, through connections, to get a fellowship for a summer school in Oxford. The official purpose of the fellowship was to learn English, and I remember an excellent young Englishman by the name of Alexander who did his best to correct my mispronunciations. The comparatively primitive level on which my English still functioned at the time may be gathered from an experience one evening when I strolled around Oxford. On some square I found a public speaker who harangued a sparse audience. I understood him to advertise some kind of cheese, and it took me some time to realize that he was rather propagating Jesus. The great impression of these months was a number of lectures by Gilbert Murray. The impression was overwhelming: it was my first introduction to the style of distinguished English scholarship at its best.

10

American Influence

I have already referred to my year in New York, in which one important influence came through the younger men surrounding Thomas Hunt Morgan. This year in New York was possible because at that time the Rockefeller Foundation extended research fellowships to European students under the title of the Laura Spellman Rockefeller Fellowships. I was one of the first recipients, so far as I know the first from Austria, and I had this fellowship for three years. The first year I spent in New York at Columbia University. In the second year I went for one semester to Harvard and the second semester to Wisconsin. The third year I spent in Paris.

These two years in America brought the great break in my intellectual development. My interests, though far ranging, were still provincial, inasmuch as the location in Central Europe was not favorable to an understanding of the larger world beyond Continental Europe. At Columbia University I took courses with Franklin Henry Giddings the sociologist, John Dewey, Irwin Edman, John Wesley the economist, John Whittier Macmahon in public administration, and I was overwhelmed by a new world of which hitherto I had hardly suspected the existence. The most important influence came from the library. During the year in New York, I started working through the history of English philosophy and its expansion into American thought. My studies were strongly motivated and helped by Dewey and Edman. I discovered English and American common sense philosophy. More immediately, the impact came through Dewey's recent book, *Human Na-*

ture and Conduct, which was based on the English common
sense tradition. From there, I worked back to Thomas Reid and
Sir William Hamilton. This English and Scottish conception of
common sense as a human attitude that incorporates a philosopher's attitude toward life without the philosopher's technical apparatus, and inversely the understanding of Classic
and Stoic philosophy as the technical, analytical elaboration of
the common sense attitude, has remained a lasting influence
in my understanding both of common sense and Classic philosophy. It was during this time that I got the first inkling of
what the continued tradition of Classic philosophy on the
common sense level, without necessarily the technical apparatus of an Aristotle, could mean for the intellectual climate
and the cohesion of a society.

Precisely this tradition of common sense I now recognized
to be the factor that was signally absent from the German
social scene, and not so well developed in France as it was in
England and America. In retrospect, I would say that the ab-
sence of political institutions rooted in an intact common
sense tradition is a fundamental defect of the German political
structure that still has not been overcome. When I look at the
contemporary German scene, with its frenetic debate between
positivists, neo-Marxists, and neo-Hegelians, it is the same
scene that I observed when I was a student in the 1920s in the
Weimar Republic; the intellectual level, however, has become
abnormally mediocre. The great figures engaged pro and con in
the analysis of philosophical problems in the 1920s—men like
Max Scheler, Karl Jaspers, Martin Heidegger, Alfred Weber,
Karl Mannheim—have disappeared from the scene and have
not been replaced by men of comparable stature and competence. During my year in New York, I began to sense that
American society had a philosophical background far superior
in range and existential substance, though not always in articulation, to anything that I found represented in the methodological environment in which I had grown up.

During the year at Columbia, when I took the courses of
Giddings and Dewey and read their work, I became aware of
the categories of social substance in the English-speaking

world. John Dewey's category was *likemindedness*, which I found was the term used by the King James Bible to translate the New Testament term *homonoia*. That was the first time I became aware of the problem of *homonoia*, about which I knew extremely little at the time, because my knowledge of Classic philosophy was still quite insufficient and my knowledge of Christian problems practically nonexistent. Only later, when I had learned Greek and was able to read the texts in the original, did I become aware of the fundamental function of such categories for determining what the substance of society really is. Giddings' term was the *consciousness of kind*. Though I did not know very much about the background of these problems, I remember becoming aware that Giddings was intending the same problem as John Dewey but preferred a terminology that would not make visible the connection of the problem with Classic and Christian traditions. It was his attempt to transform the *homonoia*, in the sense of a community of the spirit, into something innocuous like a community of kind in a biological sense.

This year at Columbia was supplemented by the second year in which the strongest impression at Harvard was the newly arrived Alfred North Whitehead. Of course, I could understand only a very small portion of what Whitehead said in his lectures, and I had to work myself into the cultural and historical background of his book that came out at the time, *The Adventures of Ideas*. But it brought to my attention that there was such a background into which I had to work myself more intensely if I wanted to understand Anglo-Saxon civilization. The occasion for expanding my knowledge offered itself in the second semester of the year 1925–26, when I went to Wisconsin. I had become aware of the work of John R. Commons at Columbia, because during that year his *Human Nature and Property* was published. Thomas Reed Powell, who at that time was still at Columbia (the next year he went to Harvard), had commented upon Commons' work. In Wisconsin I got into what I considered at the time, with my still limited knowledge, to be the real, authentic America. It was represented by John R. Commons, who took on for me the shape of a

Lincolnesque figure, strongly connected with economic and political problems both on the state and national level, and with particular accent on the labor problem. In that environment in Wisconsin, with a man like Selig Perlman as the historian of labor and the young people who worked with Commons and Perlman as fellow students, I acquired my first enlarged knowledge of the importance of the U.S. Supreme Court and its opinions as the source of political culture in America. This experience of Wisconsin became a strong factor in my later career. When I came permanently to America in 1938, I wanted to go into the teaching of American government as the core for understanding American political culture; and since as a newly arrived foreigner I would not be admitted to teach American government at an Eastern university, I went to the South where reservations in this respect were somewhat less strong.

This account of my American experience would be incomplete without mentioning the strong influence of George Santayana. I never met him, but I got acquainted with his work in New York, partly through the suggestion of Irwin Edman. I studied his work with care and still have in my library the books that I bought that year in New York. To me, Santayana was a revelation concerning philosophy, comparable to the revelation I received at the same time through common sense philosophy. Here was a man with a vast background of philosophical knowledge, sensitive to the problems of the spirit without accepting a dogma, and not interested at all in neo-Kantian methodology. Gradually I found out about Lucretian materialism as a motivating experience in his thought, and this was of considerable importance for my understanding later, in Paris, the French poet Paul Valéry and his Lucretian motivation. Santayana and Valéry have remained for me the two great representatives of an almost mystical skepticism that in fact is not materialism at all. The emotional impact of this discovery was so strong and lasting that in the 1960s, when I had an opportunity to travel in southern France, I went to see the Cimetière Marin in Cette where Valéry is buried overlooking the Mediterranean.

The results of these two years in America precipitated my book *Über die Form des amerikanischen Geistes*. The various chapters correspond to the several areas of literature and history that I had worked through. The chapter on "Time and Existence" reflects my studies in the English philosophy of consciousness and its comparison with the German theory of consciousness represented by Edmund Husserl. The chapter on George Santayana gives my summary of the work and philosophical personality of Santayana as I understood it at the time. A further chapter on "Puritan Mysticism" is the result of my studies on Jonathan Edwards—even in retrospect I must say it is a good essay. The next chapter on "Anglo-American Analytical Theory of Law," about fifty pages, reflects my study of this area that in English and American civilization is the counterpart to the "norm logic" of Kelsen in the Continental European theory of law. And the last chapter on "John R. Commons" reflects my understanding of the work and personality of John R. Commons as well as the fervent admiration that I had for him.

This literary work in which I assembled the results of the two American years does not, however, give a full understanding of the importance these years had in my life. The great event was the fact of being thrown into a world for which the great neo-Kantian methodological debates, which I considered the most important things intellectually, were of no importance. Instead, there was the background of the great political foundation of 1776 and 1789, and of the unfolding of this founding act through a political and legal culture primarily represented by the lawyers' guild and the Supreme Court. There was the strong background of Christianity and Classical culture that was so signally fading out, if not missing, in the methodological debates in which I had grown up as a student. In brief, there was a world in which this other world in which I had grown up was intellectually, morally, and spiritually irrelevant. That there should be such a plurality of worlds had a devastating effect on me. The experience broke for good (at least I hope it did) my Central European or generally European provincialism without letting me fall into an American provincialism. I gained an understanding in these years of the plurality of human possibilities realized in various civilizations, as an immediate experience, an *expérience vécue,* which hitherto had been accessible to me only through the comparative study of civilizations as I found them in Max Weber, in Spengler, and later in Toynbee. The immediate effect was that upon my return to Europe certain phenomena that were of the greatest importance in the intellectual and ideological context of Central Europe, for instance the work of Martin Heidegger, whose famous *Sein und Zeit* I read in 1928, no longer had any effect on me. It just ran off, because I had been immunized against this whole context of philosophizing through my time in America and especially in Wisconsin. The priorities and relations of importance between various theories had been fundamentally changed, and so far as I can see changed for the better.

11

Concerning the Year in France

After the two years in America, the Rockefeller Foundation
was kind enough to extend the Laura Spellman Rockefeller
Memorial Fellowship for another year to continue my studies
in France. I accepted the opportunity with the idea of enlarging
my horizon by living in France for a year and finding out first-
hand what points in French culture were relevant for a political scientist. The field for studies was wide open. I attended
courses in the law school, especially with a French economist
named Aftalion, and I attended the lectures of the famous Léon
Brunschvicg, the Pascal scholar. In the beginning my studies
were somewhat hampered because I had a reading knowledge
of French but not a really good knowledge of a more complicated vocabulary. I remember reading the *Trois Contes* by
Gustave Flaubert, which was quite an ordeal because Flaubert's vocabulary is enormous, and I had to use a dictionary in
practically every sentence. But reading authors who have a
large vocabulary is the only way of building up a knowledge of
a language.

At the time, there was an irresistible attraction in Paris—
that is, the flood of Russian refugees. I happened to get acquainted with quite a few of them and understood the necessity of learning Russian in order to have access to the political
materials. So I started on it with Konstantin V. Mochulski and
G. Lozinski as teachers. The work with these two excellent
philologists continued practically through the whole year, and
I got far enough to be able to read Dostoevsky. Unfortunately, I
have forgotten most of what I learned because in the practice of

my work I had later too little occasion to deal with Russian sources.

But the main area of studies, of course, was French literature and philosophy. Good guides for introducing myself to the problems of these fields were the works of Albert Thibaudet on Mallarmé and Valéry, and of René Lalou on the history of French literature in general and on the history of the novel in particular. I acquired in this year in Paris a practically complete set of the important French prose literature from *La Princesse de Clèves* by Madame de La Fayette to the work of Marcel Proust, whose last volumes of *A la Recherche du temps perdu* were coming out at the time. Marcel Proust, like Flaubert, was an inestimable source for enriching my French vocabulary. René Lalou's *De Descartes à Proust* was of fundamental importance for my understanding of the continuity of French intellectual history. Here I found the French history of consciousness that runs parallel to the history of consciousness in English and American philosophy from the eighteenth century to the present.

Through both Thibaudet and Lalou my attention was directed especially to Mallarmé and Valéry. At this time I assembled my almost complete collection of the works of Paul Valéry, several of them in first editions that now have become valuable. I had occasion to see Valéry when he gave an after-dinner talk at some meeting connected with the League of Nations. What interested me most about him at the time, besides the fact that he was a great artist, was his Lucretian philosophy, which I understood as a parallel phenomenon to the Lucretianism of George Santayana. The poem with which I fell in love particularly was the "Cimetière Marin."

The opportunity of spending a year in Paris of course was also used, so far as means permitted, to see the surroundings. I remember my first great impression of Chartres and a trip in summer to the remnants of the monasteries in Normandy.

In the background, of course, were my studies in the French theory of law, especially of Léon Duguit. At that time I got my first acquaintance with the French problem of *solidarité*. Curiously enough, I was not yet attracted to the work of Henri

Bergson, though I was already familiar with his *Matière et Mémoire* and his *Essai sur les données immédiates de la conscience*. My real interest in Bergson only grew with the publication of his *Les deux sources de la morale et de la religion* in 1932. A special area of interest became the French *mémoires* literature. I remember reading with fascination the memoirs of the Cardinal de Retz, which gave me an introduction to the politics of the seventeenth century. Perhaps because of their size the memoirs of Saint-Simon interested me somewhat less. The Retz memoirs were to me especially important because they described one of the great conspiracies that were characteristic of the seventeenth century. I studied the parallel cases of the Wallenstein conspiracy, of the conspiracy of the Fiesco in Genoa, and of the conspiracy of the Spaniards in Venice. One of the *mémoires* I read at the time were those of the duc de La Rochefoucauld, which gave me the transition to the philosophy of the *moralistes*. In addition to La Rochefoucauld, I read the marquise de Vauvenargues and found out about the line of influence that goes from the French *moralistes* to Nietzsche.

I was again in Paris in 1934 for several weeks. At this time I was interested in the French sixteenth century and especially in the work of Jean Bodin. I collected materials for a comprehensive study of Bodin's work and in fact wrote it later to form part of the *History of Political Ideas*, but it has never been published. At that time, I worked through the catalogue of the Bibliothèque Nationale on French publications on the history and politics of the sixteenth century. So far as I remember, I had every single item in the catalogue in hand at least once, and on this occasion I became aware of the enormous influence that the Mongol invasions and the events of the fifteenth century, especially the temporary victory of Tamerlane over Bayezid, had as a model of the political process in the sixteenth century. Practically every author of importance dealt with these events, which were completely outside the normal experience of politics in the West and introduced an inexplicable rise to power, which affected the very existence of Western civilization, as a factor into world history. This experience of the Turkish Ottoman threat and its temporary interruption through the victory of Tamerlane were observed by the humanists and entered into the conception in Machiavelli's *Prince* of the man who can rise to power by his own virtue. Some of the voluminous materials gathered at the time I published in an article on "Das Timurbild der Humanisten" in 1937, which I later had reprinted in my *Anamnesis* of 1966. The influence of these events on Machiavelli, and especially on his fictitious biography of Castruccio Castracani, I published in my article on Machiavelli's background in the *Review of Politics* in 1951. But considerable piles of materials and the connection with the work of Bodin have never been published.

In the same year, 1934, I spent some weeks in London exploring the resources of the Warburg Institute, which had already moved there from Hamburg. This was my first contact with alchemy, astrology, and the complicated gnostic symbolism of the Renaissance. The materials collected on that occasion were incorporated in a chapter on "Astrological Politics" for my *History of Political Ideas*, which, as I said, has not been published. This first acquaintance was the basis for my further interest in astrology and alchemy that developed much later and helped me to gain some understanding of certain continuities in Western intellectual history from the Middle Ages through the Renaissance into the present.

12

Return to Vienna

After my return from the three years under the Rockefeller Fellowship, I began to concentrate on writing publications that would lead to my habilitation and ultimately to a professorship. The first thing I finished was the book that was published under the title *Über die Form des amerikanischen Geistes*, which came out in 1928. Then I looked for further occupation. I began to develop a system of *Staatslehre* and actually wrote sections dealing with the theory of law and the theory of power. Then there should have been a third part on political ideas, but when I came to that third part I discovered that I knew nothing whatsoever about political ideas and had to give up the project of a *Staatslehre*. I began to concentrate on acquiring knowledge of specific ideas for the purpose of analyzing the problem of the so-called ideas with the concrete materials in hand.

The results of this work were my studies on the race question. The National Socialist movement obviously was in political ascendancy; and though one could not yet foresee that it would come to power, the debate about races, the Jewish problem, etc., went on all the time. The material suggested itself for treatment, resulting in my two volumes on the race question. Into these volumes I also incorporated my recently acquired and now elaborated knowledge of biological theory. On that occasion I found out that a political theory, especially when it was to be applicable to the analysis of ideologies, had to be based on Classic and Christian philosophy. As the first chapter of my volume on *Rasse und Staat* shows, I adopted at the time the philosophical anthropology of Max Scheler, as expressed in his recent publication *Die Stellung des Menschen im Kosmos*. It proved sufficient for the purpose of analyzing the race problem; its defects were of no importance to the issue at hand, though I discovered them later when I started on my original work on Classic philosophy.

While working on the race problem, I became convinced that I had to be able to read the Classic authors, that is, Plato and Aristotle, if I wanted to become a competent political scientist. I started to learn Greek with the help of a man about my age, Hermann Bodek, a minor member of the *Stefan-George-Kreis* and an excellent classics philologist. Bodek introduced me to the secrets of Greek grammar and to the reading of complicated philosophical texts. I remember that in the course of the six months in which I took lessons from him I made my first translations of the poems of Parmenides. The acquisition of that knowledge was of course fundamental for my later work, not only so far as my knowledge of Greek philosophy was concerned, but for understanding fundamentally that one cannot deal with materials unless one can read them. That sounds trivial, but as I later found out it is a truth not only neglected but hotly contested by a good number of persons who are employed by our colleges and who, with the greatest of ease, talk about Plato and Aristotle, or Thomas and Augustine, or Dante and Cervantes, or Rabelais or Goethe, without being able to read a line of the authors on whom they pontificate.

The years in Austria, beginning with 1933, were emotionally packed by the political events of the time. I had become a *Privatdozent* in 1929, and I received the title of Associate Professor in 1936, but neither of these dignities was connected with any material support. During these years I was an assistant for constitutional and administrative law at the Law Faculty, first to Kelsen and later to Merkl. That gave a very modest income. I remember it started at one hundred schillings a month. At the time I left in 1938 it was two hundred fifty schillings, which was about $50. Even if you quadruple the sum in view of the dollar's devaluation, it was not more than $250 per month, on which I had to pay taxes. Everything else necessary for living I had to gain through freelance writing, teaching, and so forth. One might say I have always been an independent entrepreneur.

The situation in Vienna tightened through the events of the Civil War in 1934. On that occasion, the disastrous disintegration of Central European society through the ideologists became obvious. There was an Austrian government that firmly resisted any advance of National Socialism but was endangered in its effectiveness by the opposition, because the Social Democratic party, due to its Marxist ideology, did not want to admit that a small country like the Austrian Republic had to accommodate itself to the political pressures of the time. The Austrian veering toward Mussolini as a protection against the worse evil of Hitler apparently was beyond the comprehension of ardent Marxists, who could do nothing but yell "Fascism."

As a matter of fact, as a student in the 1920s I had been, though not a member of the organized party, by inclination a Social Democrat like most of my friends. And in the election of 1920 I voted for the Social Democratic party. When the internal tensions began to grow in developing an Austrian nationalism that would resist National Socialism as well as Communism, the split in the population increased, but I did not participate in it because in the critical three years 1924 to 1927 I was not in Austria. I still remember that the great clash with the "Brand of the Justizpalast" in 1927 occurred just when I set out from Paris, with some of my American friends, for a trip to Normandy. Only when I returned to Austria in the fall of 1927 did I again become interested in Austrian politics.

For two reasons I veered more in the direction of the Christian Socialist government. In the first place, the Christian Socialist politicians represented the traditions of European culture, whereas the Marxists at least overtly did not. I say at least overtly, because in fact even the ardent Marxists were living in the Austrian tradition, which was eminently democratic and habit-forming. But inevitably Marxist ideology caused difficulties, when the party program had an explicit passage saying that the Social Democratic party would abide by democratic procedures until it had gained the majority of votes. Once the majority had been gained, the Socialist revolution would start: no return to the nefariousness of a capitalist democracy would be permitted but would rather be resisted by force. What struck me most at the time was the stupidity of ideologists as represented by the leaders of the Social Democratic party. While I agreed with them regarding economic and social politics, the silliness of their apocalyptic dream in face of the impending Hitlerian apocalypse was simply too much to stomach. My attitude toward the Social Democracy at the time can be identified with the position taken by Karl Kraus. Ideological intellectuals who survived the disaster have not yet forgiven Kraus for being too intelligent to sympathize with their foolishness. Of course, they have not forgiven me, either.

The result of these years of tension after 1933 was my study on *Die Autoritäre Staat*, published in 1936. It was my first major attempt to penetrate the role of ideologies, left and right, in the contemporary situation and to understand that an authoritarian state that would keep radical ideologists in check was the best possible defense of democracy. My theoretical attitude in these matters at the time was not very different from the attitude later expressed by Supreme Court Justice Robert H. Jackson, in the *Terminiello* case of 1949 (after he got acquainted with European radical ideologies as a member of the Nuremburg court), in the formula that democracy is "not a suicide pact."

13

Anschluss and Emigration

A profound emotional shock came in the critical moments of the destruction of Austria. I would have left Vienna long before 1938 if I had not assumed that Austria was safe in its defense against National Socialism. On the basis of my historically founded political knowledge, I considered it impossible that the Western democracies would permit the annexation of Austria by Hitler, because the event obviously would be the first of a series that would culminate in a world war. The German occupation of Austria would create a strategic situation that made the conquest of Czechoslovakia possible; and the conquest of Czechoslovakia would consolidate a Central European position that made a war with the Western powers potentially victorious. It came as a great surprise to me that the Western powers did nothing. From a friend who was at the time working in Rome and had friends in the Italian foreign ministry, I learned that on the night of the invasion Mussolini was engaged in frantic telephone conversations with the English government pleading for common action, which, however, was rejected. I remember that the events caused in me a state of unlimited fury. In the wake of the Austrian occupation by Hitler, I even for a moment contemplated joining the National Socialists, because those rotten swine who called themselves democrats—meaning the Western democracies—certainly deserved to be conquered and destroyed if they were capable of such criminal idiocy. But the character development of the past would not permit this extreme step. Reason got the better after several hours of such fury, and I prepared my emigration. That was necessary, because I had never made any secret of my anti-National Socialist attitude, and of course I was immediately fired from my position at the university.

Preparing to emigrate brought the usual odd details that are connected with such an enterprise. Above all, I had to acquire some money outside Austria, because the export of money was prohibited. I had a Swiss friend who was a journalist in Vienna, reporting for Swiss newspapers, with whom I arranged to pay his income in Austria while he left the equivalent value in Swiss francs with his lawyer in Zurich. The money accumulated and became the basis for living a number of months in Zurich before I could get my immigration visa from the American consulate.

The emigration plan almost miscarried. Though I was politically an entirely unimportant figure, and the important ones had to be caught first, my turn came at last. Just when we had nearly finished our preparations and my passport was with the police in order to get the exit visa, the Gestapo appeared at my apartment to confiscate the passport. Fortunately, I was not at home, and my wife (Lissy Onken Voegelin) was delighted to tell them that the passport was with the police for the purpose of getting the exit visa, which satisfied the Gestapo. We were able, through friends, to get the passport, including the exit visa, from the police before the Gestapo got it—that all in one day. On the same day, in the evening, with two bags, I caught a train to Zurich, trembling on the way that the Gestapo after all would find out about me and arrest me at the border. But apparently even the Gestapo was not as efficient as my wife and I in these matters, and I got through unarrested. My wife stayed with her parents, with a Gestapo guard in front of the apartment waiting for me to show up again. My wife knew that I had escaped when the Gestapo guard was withdrawn, and about twenty minutes later my telegram arrived from Zurich telling her that I had arrived there.

But that was only the beginning of odd events. In Zurich, I had to wait for a nonquota immigration visa extended to scholars who had been offered a job in the United States. My friends at Harvard—Haberler, Schumpeter, and, in a very decisive function as head of the Department of Government, Arthur Holcombe—had provided a part-time instructorship. But I had not yet received the official letter, and I had to wait for that in order to get the American visa. In waiting for the visa, I had dealings with the American vice-consul in Zurich, a very nice Harvard boy who had grave suspicions about me. He explained that, since I was neither a Communist nor a Catholic nor a Jew, I therefore had no reason whatsoever not to be in favor of National Socialism and to be a National Socialist myself. Hence, if I was in flight the only reason must be some criminal record, and he did not want to give me a visa before the matter of my criminality was cleared up. Fortunately, in due course Holcombe's letter arrived, advising me of my appointment as a part-time instructor, and with his signature on the letter the Harvard boy in the consulate was convinced that I was in the fold, so I got my visa.

I am telling this incident not in order to be critical of this particular vice-consul, who was as innocent of political problems, and especially human problems, as such people happen to be. Let me tell, therefore, a similar incident that occurred more than twenty years later, in the 1960s. The occasion was a meeting in Salzburg where Ernst Bloch, the Marxist philosopher, and I were invited to lecture. Our wives were there, too. At a dinner party the ladies got into conversation, and Mrs. Bloch inquired cautiously why we happened to have come to America, too, because after all we were not Jews; and she asked whether I had been a Communist. My wife explained that I had not been a Communist either. Whereupon Mrs. Bloch asked her, "Well then, why couldn't he stay in Austria?" That anybody could be anti-National Socialist without being motivated by an ideological counterposition or because he was a Jew is indeed, so far as my experience goes, inconceivable to most people whom I know in the academic world.

14

Concerning Ideology, Personal Politics, and Publications

As the anecdotes just related show, my personal attitude in politics, and especially with regard to National Socialism, is frequently misunderstood, because entirely too many people who express themselves in public cannot understand that resistance to National Socialism can have other reasons than partisan motives. My reasons for hating National Socialism from the time I first got acquainted with it in the 1920s can be reduced to very elementary reactions. There was in the first place the influence of Max Weber. One of the virtues that he demanded of a scholar was "intellektuelle Rechtschaffenheit," which can be translated as intellectual honesty. I cannot see any reason why anybody should work in the social sciences, and generally in the sciences of man, unless he honestly wants to explore the structure of reality. Ideologies, whether Positivist, or Marxist, or National Socialist, indulge in constructions that are intellectually not tenable. That raises the question of why people who otherwise are not quite stupid, and who have the secondary virtues of being quite honest in their daily affairs, indulge in intellectual dishonesty as soon as they touch science. That ideology is a phenomenon of intellectual dishonesty is beyond a doubt, because the various ideologies after all have been submitted to criticism, and anybody who is willing to read the literature knows that they are not tenable, and why. If one adheres to them nevertheless, the prima facie assumption must be that he is intellectually dishonest. The overt phenomenon of intellectual dishonesty then raises the question of why a man will indulge in it. That is a general problem that in my later years required complicated research to ascertain the nature, causes, and persistence of states of alienation. More immediately, on the overt level that imposed itself, it caused my opposition to any ideologies—Marxist, Fascist, National Socialist, what you will—because they were incompatible with science in the rational sense of critical analysis. I again refer back to Max Weber as the great thinker who brought that problem to my attention; and I still maintain today that nobody who is an ideologist can be a competent social scientist.

As a consequence, partisan problems are of secondary importance; they come under the head of ideologists fighting each other. That, however, is not an entirely new phenomenon. I had to note the same problem in my studies on the intellectual battles in the Reformation of the sixteenth century. There I summarized the problem in the formula that there are intellectual situations where everybody is so wrong that it is enough to maintain the opposite in order to be at least partially right. The exploration of these structures helps to understand the meaning of "public opinion," but these structures certainly have nothing to do with science.

Because of this attitude I have been called every conceivable name by partisans of this or that ideology. I have in my files documents labeling me a Communist, a Fascist, a National Socialist, an old Liberal, a new Liberal, a Jew, a Catholic, a Protestant, a Platonist, a neo-Augustinian, a Thomist, and of course a Hegelian—not to forget that I was supposedly strongly influenced by Huey Long. This list I consider of some importance, because the various characterizations of course always name the pet bête noire of the respective critic and give, therefore, a very good picture of the intellectual destruction and corruption that characterize the contemporary academic world. Understandably, I have never answered such criticisms; critics of this type can become objects of inquiry, but they cannot be partners in a discussion.

A further reason for my hatred of National Socialism and other ideologies is quite a primitive one. I have an aversion to killing people for the fun of it. What the fun is, I did not quite understand at the time, but in the intervening years the ample exploration of revolutionary consciousness has cast some light on this matter. The fun consists in gaining a pseudo-identity through asserting one's power, optimally by killing somebody—a pseudo-identity that serves as a substitute for the human self that has been lost. Some of these problems I touched upon in my study on the "Eclipse of Reality," published in 1970. A good example of the type of self that has to kill other people in order to regain in an *Ersatzform* what it has lost is the famous Saint-Juste, who says that Brutus either has to kill other people or kill himself. The matter has been explored by Albert Camus, and the murderous equanimity of the intellectuals who have lost their self and try to regain it by becoming pimps for this or that murderous totalitarian power is excellently exemplified by Maurice Merleau-Ponty's *Humanisme et Terreur* (1947). I have no sympathy whatsoever with such characters and have never hesitated to characterize them as "murderous swine."

The third motif that I can ascertain in my hatred against ideologies is that of a man who likes to keep his language clean. If anything is characteristic of ideologies and ideological thinkers, it is the destruction of language, sometimes on the level of intellectual jargon of a high level of complication, sometimes on a vulgarian level. From my personal experience with various ideologists of a Hegelian or Marxist type, I have the impression that a good number of men of considerable intellectual energy who otherwise would be Marxists prefer to be Hegelians because Hegel is so much more complicated. This is a difference not of any profound conviction but of what I would compare to the taste of a man who prefers chess to pinochle. Hegel is more complicated, and one can easily spend a lifetime exploring the possibilities of interpreting reality from this or that corner of the Hegelian system, without of course ever touching on the premises that are wrong—and perhaps without ever finding out that there *are* premises that are wrong. In conversations with Hegelians, I have quite regularly found that as soon as one touches on Hegelian premises the Hegelian refuses to enter into the argument and assures you that you cannot understand Hegel unless you accept his premises. That, of course, is perfectly true—but if the premises are wrong, everything that follows from them is wrong, too, and a good ideologist therefore has to prevent their discussion. In the case of Hegel, that is comparatively easy, because Hegel was a first-rate thinker and knew the history of philosophy. Hence, if one wants to attack Hegel's premises one has to know their background in Plotinus and the neo-Platonic mysticism of the seventeenth century. Since very few people who pontificate about Hegel have any knowledge of philosophy comparable to his, the premises can easily be kept in the dark, and sometimes need not even be kept in the dark because they are, anyway, in the darkness of the ignorance of those who talk about him.

In the Marxian case, the falseness of the premises is more obvious. When Marx writes about Hegel he distorts him so badly that his honest editors cannot help being aware of the fact and expressing themselves cautiously on their findings. The editors of the *Frühschriften* of Karl Marx (Kröner, 1955), especially Siegfried Landshut, say regarding Marx's study of Hegel's *Philosophy of Law*: "Marx, if one may express oneself in this manner, by misunderstanding Hegel as it were deliberately, conceives all concepts of Hegel which are meant as predicates of the idea as statements about facts" (pp. xxv–xxvi). In my uncivilized manner as a man who does not like to murder people for the purpose of supplying intellectuals with fun, I flatly state that Marx was consciously an intellectual swindler for the purpose of maintaining an ideology that would permit him to support violent action against human beings with a show of moral indignation. I stated the problem explicitly in my inaugural lecture in Munich in 1958 [*Science, Politics, and Gnosticism* (Kösel, 1959; English ed., 1968)] and explored on that occasion the mental disturbance that lies behind such action. Marx, however, conducted his arguments on a very high intellectual level, and the surprise (with repercussions in the daily press) caused by my flat statement that he was engaged in an intellectual swindle can easily be explained in the same way as the darkness that surrounds the premises of

Hegel. The Marxian swindle concerns the flat refusal to enter into the etiological argument of Aristotle—that is, on the problem that man does not exist out of himself but out of the divine ground of all reality. Again, as distinguished from our contemporaries who pontificate on Marx, Marx himself had a very good philosophical education. He knew that the problem of etiology in human existence was the central problem of a philosophy of man; and if he wanted to destroy man's humanity by making him a "socialist man," he had to refuse to enter into the etiological problem. On this point he was, one must admit, considerably more honest than Hegel, who never quoted the arguments into which he refused to enter. But the effect is the same as in the case of Hegel, because contemporary critics, of course, know about Aristotle and the etiological argument just as much as they know about Hegel's neo-Platonic background—which is to say, exactly nothing. The general deculturation of the academic and intellectual world in Western civilization furnishes the background for the social dominance of opinions that would have been laughed out of court in the late Middle Ages or the Renaissance.

When we advance beyond Marx to the ideological epigones of the late nineteenth and of the twentieth century, we are already far below the intellectual level that formed the background even of Marx. And here comes in my particular hatred of ideologists because they vulgarize the intellectual debate and give to public discussion the distinctly ochlocratic coloring that today has reached the point of considering as fascist or authoritarian even a reference to the facts of political and intellectual history that must be known if one wants to discuss the problems that come up in political debate. The radical condemnation of historical and philosophical knowledge must be recognized as an important factor in the social environment, because it is dominated by persons who cannot even be called intellectual crooks because their level of consciousness is much too low to be aware of their objective crookedness, but who must rather be characterized as functional illiterates with a strong desire for personal aggrandizement.

These observations then bring us down to the level of National Socialism. It is extremely difficult to engage in a critical discussion of National Socialist ideas, as I found out when I gave my semester course on "Hitler and the Germans" in 1964 in Munich, because in National Socialist and related documents, we are still farther below the level on which rational argument is possible than in the case of Hegel and Marx. In order to deal with rhetoric of this type, one must first develop a philosophy of language, going into the problems of symbolization on the basis of the philosophers' experience of humanity and of the perversion of such symbols on the vulgarian level by people who are utterly unable to read a philosopher's work. A person on this level—which I characterize as the vulgarian and, so far as it becomes socially relevant, as the ochlocratic level—again, is not admissible to the position of a partner in discussion but can only be an object of scientific research. These vulgarian and ochlocratic problems must not be taken lightly; one cannot simply not take notice of them. They are serious problems of life and death because the vulgarians create and dominate the intellectual climate in which the rise to power of figures like Hitler is possible. I would say, therefore, that in the German case the destroyers of the German language on the literary and journalistic level, characterized and analyzed over more than thirty years by Karl Kraus in the volumes of *Die Fackel*, were the true criminals who were guilty of the National Socialist atrocities, which were possible only when the social environment had been so destroyed by the vulgarians that a person who was truly representative of this vulgarian spirit could rise to power.

These motivations were perfectly clear to me at the time, but clarity about their direction did not mean clarity about the implications in detail. The intellectual apparatus for dealing with the highly complex phenomena of intellectual deformation, perversion, crookedness, and vulgarization did not yet exist, and studies to create this apparatus were required. Into this context belong the studies that I published under the title *Die politischen Religionen* in 1938. When I spoke of the *politischen Religionen*, I conformed to the usage of a literature that interpreted ideological movements as a variety of religions. Representative for this literature was Louis Rougier's successful volume on *Les Mystiques politiques*. The interpretation is not all wrong, but I would no longer use the term *religions* because it is too vague and already deforms the real problem of experiences by mixing them with the further problem of dogma or doctrine. Moreover, in *Die politischen Religionen* I still pooled together such phenomena as the spiritual movement of Ikhnaton, the medieval theories of spiritual and temporal power, apocalypses, the *Leviathan* of Hobbes, and certain National Socialist symbolisms. A more adequate treatment would have required far-reaching differentiations between these various phenomena. The book was just coming from the printer in March of 1938, when the National Socialist occupation of Austria occurred. The publishing house of Berman-Fischer was an inevitable target of the occupation forces, and the whole edition was confiscated at the publisher and never reached the public. Later I learned that a few copies had gone into commerce; apparently various National Socialist agencies received copies from the Gestapo, and these began circulating after World War II.

The volume on *Der autoritäre Staat*, published in 1936 in Vienna, was on the whole a piece of forced labor. I had been habilitated as a *Privatdozent* for sociology and wanted to expand my *venia legendi* to political science. For that purpose I had to write a new book of an undoubtedly political science nature and, if possible, on a subject related to Austrian politics. Material was there aplenty, because the 1930s were the period of the general resistance against National Socialism, of the Civil War of 1934, the murder of Engelbert Dollfuss, and ultimately the creation of a corporate constitution. The new authoritarian constitution and its background were a suitable subject for treatment because at that time nobody else paid any attention to these matters.

The book is somewhat heterogeneous. In the first part, I dealt with the symbols *total* and *authoritarian*. Again, I should like to stress that at the time nobody else dealt with problems of this nature, and no intellectual apparatus for treating these topical terms had been created. I developed on that occasion the distinction between *topoi* and concepts. This distinction is basic for an adequate treatment of language problems in politics. Conventionally, whatever pops up as a language symbol in politics is simply accepted as such and enters the vague realm of political ideas. The first step in getting some rational order into this vague mass is to be clear about what constitutes theory (this question had already motivated my study of classical political philosophy) and in what way the concepts of theory differ from other language symbols, which do not express the order of existence, but various disorders and deformations of concepts only half understood by illiterates on the vulgarian level. To this class of political symbols, which are definitely not theoretical concepts, belong such symbols as *total* and *authoritarian*.

My interpretation of the Austrian authoritarian state derived considerable help from Maurice Hauriou's institutionalism. Moreover, I had already been branching out into various areas of the history of philosophy, and I was able to recognize in the assumption of a collective entity that would justify the treatment of its members as subordinate beings who had to conform to the ideas of whoever represented the collective entity parallels to the Averroeist conception of the *intellectus unus* of which the mind of human beings is no more than a spark. I am not sure I was quite conscious of the importance of this finding. Certainly I already understood that the transfer of the conception of an *intellectus unus* to a world-immanent entity called *nation*, or *race*, and its representatives was lethal to man's humanity. And I certainly was aware of the very serious split in the interpretation of Aristotle's psychology that took place in the Middle Ages between Averroes and Thomas, my preference being on the side of Thomas rather than of the Averroizing thinkers. A small bit of the materials that I worked through at that time was later published in my study on "Siger de Brabant" in 1944.

The reaction to this find of mine had a funny side effect. Since Averroes happened to be an Arab, and Arabs are Semites, and Semites in the end are Jews, certain thinkers close to the National Socialist regime like Carl Schmitt seriously doubted that the National Socialist collectivism had anything to do with such dirty Semitic origins. An important element in this first part was also my first clear understanding of Rousseau's variety of collectivism. At the time I did not go very far in the analysis, only a few pages, but it is the problem that later was worked out splendidly by J. L. Talmon in his *Origins of Totalitarian Democracy* (1952).

The second part of the book gave a survey of Austrian problems of constitution making, in the historical perspective since 1848. It was the occasion for me to learn something about the background of constitutional problems in the Austro-Hungarian monarchy and the continuity of solutions found at the time with the problems of the Austrian Republic after 1918.

In the third part, dealing with the new constitution, I gave an extensive analysis of Kelsen's Pure Theory of Law and its connection with a specifically Austrian theory of politics. The analysis runs about fifty pages. That was the section that got me into trouble with Kelsen, because here I obviously rejected not the Pure Theory of Law, but its claim to be a substitute for a theory of politics. I had to stress the inadequacy of a theory of law for understanding political problems and the destructive consequences of the claim that one should, or could, not deal scientifically with political problems. My relationship with Kelsen was never the same after that, and years later, in America, after *The New Science of Politics* came out in 1952, he wrote an elaborate book-length critique crushing me thoroughly. However, Kelsen's critique, which he was kind enough to let me see in manuscript, was never published, perhaps because I conveyed to him directly through a letter in cautious form, and through common friends more outspokenly, that his understanding of the historical and philosophical problems involved in the matter was inadequate and a publication would damage his prestige rather than mine. Since *Der autoritäre Staat* came out in 1936, and its sale was stopped in 1938 when the Nazis occupied Austria, it did not receive much attention at the time. Nor did it later, because during the Russian conquest of Vienna one of the bombs fell, of all places, on the Springer publishing house, and the whole edition was burned in the cellar.

15

Concerning Emigration in 1938

As I explained previously, I barely escaped from Austria. The Gestapo was about to confiscate my passport, and that would have meant the end of any possibility of emigration short of a secret border crossing. But the Gestapo's attention also had its funny side. For instance, in the general survey of university personnel, a Gestapo officer came to our home and searched around my desk, drawers, and bookcases in order to see what I did. He was a young man in his mid-twenties, and when we got friendly he told me that he was originally a lawyer from Hamburg. First he inspected my desk for incriminating material. At the time, since I had been fired and had nothing to do but prepare for my emigration, I had complete leisure for the exploration of complicated problems. I was working at the time on questions of empire, and my desk was piled high with treatises on Byzantium, several of them in French and English. So he thumbed through this Byzantine empire literature; and after a while he remarked that he was in charge of inspecting all of the professors in the Law School, and that my desk was the first he had seen that looked like the desk of a scholar. The atmosphere became more relaxed. He had to take with him some incriminating evidence concerning my political interests. I had of course standing on my shelves the principal sources of a political nature: Hitler's *Mein Kampf*; Kurt von Schuschnigg's book, *Dreimal Österreich*; Mussolini's *Dottrina del Fascismo*; and Marx's *Communist Manifesto*. So he took away Schuschnigg and Marx. I protested that this would give an unfair impression of my political interests, which were strictly impartial, and suggested that he take along Hitler's *Mein Kampf*. But he refused, and that is how I kept my copy of a very early edition. But by that time we had already become more friendly. Because he also had to take with him some of my own books, such as *Über die Form des amerikanischen Geistes* and those on the race question, I suggested that it would not be nice to take the good hard-cover copies, and he could take as well the volumes of page proofs. He was agreeable and was satisfied with the page proofs, so I could keep the hard-cover editions, which I still have.

When he came in, my wife, who is a very orderly lady, wanted to take his coat, which he had thrown over a chair, and hang it in a closet. Whereupon he yelled, "Don't touch it! There is my revolver in it."

But what had to be considered due process of law under the now valid statutes was on the whole observed, and while I was apparently a target of some interest my wife was not. Besides, when I left she could stay with her parents, who were National Socialists and had a huge picture of Hitler in their living room. Of course, as soon as I had left on the evening of the day when the Gestapo man wanted to confiscate my passport, the next morning he came back in order to ask where the passport and I were. Then a guard was put in front of the house of my parents-in-law, where my wife was staying. But after I arrived in Zurich and sent a telegram, the guard disappeared, and twenty minutes later my telegram arrived. He obviously knew that I had left for good. A week later, my wife joined me in Zurich. Of course we had to leave almost everything behind, but it was possible to get some of the furniture out and, most important, the library. Certain items, however, had to be left. Again the details are more or less funny. For instance, I had to leave behind my stamp collection, which I had accumulated as a boy, this being an object of value. Books apparently were not. I know from other people that in spite of rather strict enforcement one could get a lot of things through. I know for instance of a young lady who was an artist and who had acquired a few original prints by Dürer. In order to export objects of art, one had to get a permit, so she put the Dürer prints in among her own work. The official who examined her portfolio looked through one of these prints after another, and when he came to this or that Dürer print he said, "Well, well! You have made quite some progress as an artist," and left it at that.

16

Life in America: From Harvard to LSU

When I came to America in 1938, I had a part-time instructorship at Harvard. It had been secured through the offices especially of W. Y. (Bill) Elliot, Gottfried von Haberler, and Joseph von Schumpeter, with Arthur Holcombe, who was then chairman of the department, consenting to my appointment. This appointment, however, was strictly limited, and I still remember my first conversation with Holcombe. When I presented myself to him at Harvard, he told me with dry precision that Harvard was pleased to give me this opportunity for a year and that with the end of the year the opportunity was ended. The importance of the appointment was, in the first place, that by its means I could get the previously mentioned nonquota visa. Otherwise, I would have had to wait an indeterminate time until my turn came for an ordinary immigration visa. Second, of course, the start at Harvard was of the greatest value as a good address from which to look for a job elsewhere. During my first semester at Harvard I immediately commenced looking for a job. To that purpose, I wrote more than forty extensive letters to various universities and personalities making my desire for a job known over the country. The first immediate result was an appointment as instructor at Bennington College in Vermont for the spring term of 1939 [which involved commuting back and forth from Cambridge].

Bennington presented an entirely new experience to me, which at the time I could absorb only partially because my background knowledge of American society was still rather defective. Still, I understood that I did not want to stay in spite of a very tempting offer of an assistant professorship with a salary of $5,000 for the next year. My reason for rejecting the offer and looking for something else was the environment on the East Coast. In Bennington specifically I noticed the very strong leftist element, with a few outspoken Communists among the faculty and still more among the students. This environment was no more to my taste than the National Socialist environment that I just had left. More generally, I noticed that the institutions on the East Coast were overrun by refugees from Central Europe, and if I stayed in the East inevitably my status would be that of a member of the refugee group. That was not exactly to my taste either, because I had firmly decided that once I had been thrown out of Austria by the National Socialists I wanted to make the break complete and from now on be an American. This aim, however, I could hardly achieve if I was stigmatized as a member of a refugee group. Moreover, I wanted to become a political scientist. For that purpose I had to familiarize myself with American government through teaching it; and it was impossible for a foreigner to find a teaching position for American government at any of the major Eastern institutions.

So I accepted an offer from the University of Alabama. There I would come into an environment definitely free of refugees, so that adjustment and introduction to American society would at least not be externally handicapped from the beginning. Besides, I got my chance there to teach American government, and the department under the chairmanship of Roscoe Martin was more than sufficient to keep me busy for some time to come acquiring new knowledge concerning American institutions. The situation was poorly paid: I believe $2,500 for the year, roughly half of what Bennington had offered. But the general effect of adjusting myself to the new environment was indeed achieved thanks to the truly gracious reception by southerners who somewhat condescendingly enjoyed protecting an innocent from Europe. I especially want to remember Mildred Martin, the wife of the chairman, who formed a perfect friendship with my wife and helped us considerably in giving us all sorts of advice that prevented us from hurting feelings through untoward remarks.

During my two and one-half years as an assistant professor at Alabama I worked myself into American government, the Constitution, and even a certain amount of public administration. At the same time, I had to give a course on the history of political ideas. Since by then I was a member of the Southern Political Science Association and attended their meetings, some of my new colleagues became aware of my activities, and Professor Robert J. Harris, who at that time was chairman of the department at Louisiana State University, brought me to Louisiana [in 1942] as associate professor. I accepted gladly, because it improved our financial situation ever so slightly and certainly was also an improvement in environment.

That was still the time of the group who had organized the first *Southern Review*. There were, when I arrived, Robert B. Heilman and Cleanth Brooks in the Department of English, and Robert Penn Warren was still there for a year before he went to Minnesota. I also remember at least one occasion when I met Katherine Anne Porter at a party. This environment outside the Department of Government was of inestimable value, because I now had access to the interesting movement of literary criticism and gained the friendship of men who were authorities in English literature and language. I especially want to mention the help extended by Robert B. Heilman, who introduced me to certain secrets of the American history of literature and who was kind enough to help me with my difficulties in acquiring an idiomatic English style. I still remember as most important one occasion when he went through a manuscript of mine, of about twenty pages, and marked off every single idiomatic mistake, so that I had a good list of the mistakes that I had to improve generally. Heilman's analysis, I must say, was the turning point in my understanding of English and helped me gradually to acquire a moderate mastery of the language.

The friendship with Brooks and Heilman, furthermore, helped me to acquire some knowledge of the stratification in

American English by social groups. When you come as a foreigner to America, you are of course swamped by the language that all sorts of people speak around you, some of them speaking correct English, some of them local idioms, some of them a vulgarian vocabulary with all sorts of mistakes. If you do your best to adapt yourself to your environment without having any critical knowledge of what level that environment belongs to, you can easily end up at the bottom of the vulgarian scale. Heilman and Brooks were of course very much aware of such social stratification of language and helped me confirm my suspicions with regard to language I heard in the environment.

The nature of the problem can be gathered from a conversation with Cleanth Brooks. Once, when crossing the campus, I met him deep in sorrow and thought, and I asked him what worried him. He told me he had to prepare a chapter on typical mistakes for a textbook on English style that he was re-editing with Robert Penn Warren, and that it was quite a chore to find typical mistakes. I was a bit surprised and innocently told him, "Well, it is very simple to find typical mistakes. Just take any education textbook and you will find half a dozen on every page." He then explained to me that he could not use this method because educationists were far below the level of average literacy, and their mistakes could not be considered typical for an average English-speaking person. Instead, he was using sociology textbooks and sometimes had to read twenty pages of that stuff before running into a really good example. But even so, he had to worry because social scientists could not be considered to write typical English either but were below the average, though not as far below as educationists.

This is the type of stratification of which I had gradually to become aware in order to achieve a moderately tolerable English, free of ideological jargon and free of the idiosyncracies of the vulgarian levels in the academic community.

The center of my activities was of course in the Department of Government. I had to teach two sections of American government, so I achieved my goal of teaching American government for sixteen and, including the Alabama years, for twenty years. Of considerable help in my development of the understanding of American institutions was Robert J. Harris, who became a close friend. He was a first-rate connoisseur of the Supreme Court decisions and could explain to me a good number of things that otherwise would have escaped me for a long time. To the conversations with him I owe especially an understanding of the enormous importance of procedural law in the decisions of the Supreme Court. Besides American government, I had to teach courses in comparative government, at one time, even diplomatic history, and generally, throughout the years, as my main course, the "History of Political Ideas."

17

―ֺֺֺֺֺֺֺֺ―

From Political Ideas to Symbols of Experience

This brings me to the problem of the history of ideas. In Harvard I had met Fritz Morstein-Marx, who at that time was editor of a textbook series for McGraw-Hill. He was kind enough to enlist me for a textbook of moderate size—I believe 200 to 250 pages were envisaged—for this series. That is how I got beyond teaching the history of political ideas into writing one. I started on the materials, using first, as a model of what had to be included or excluded, the *History of Political Theory* (1937) by George H. Sabine, which at the time was the standard work. But as I began working more deeply into the materials, I discovered that the treatment hitherto accorded to them was inadequate and my own knowledge of the materials quite insufficient to deal with them more adequately. I actually had to work through the literature from the Greek beginnings to the present. That is what I did over the years. This procedure, however, burst the enterprise of a small textbook for the Morstein-Marx series. I could not deliver on time, because I was still busy acquiring knowledge of sources, and the more knowledge I acquired the fatter the manuscript grew.

But that was not all. In the course of the work it became obvious that the limitation imposed on a history of ideas, the convention of having it begin with the Greek Classic philosophers and end up with some contemporary ideologies, was untenable. About some of these problems I had already found out while I was in Alabama. There I discovered that one could not very well write about the Middle Ages and their politics without knowing a good deal more about the origins of Christianity than I knew at the time, and that one could not properly understand the Christian beginnings without going into the Jewish background. So it was in Alabama that I began to study Hebrew with the local rabbi, who was also teaching Hebrew at the university. The beginnings were hard, but gradually I acquired a sufficient knowledge of grammar and vocabulary to be able to check translations and finally to make my own translations on the basis of the texts. Through these studies on the Israelite background the pattern of a history of political ideas beginning with Greek philosophy had already exploded. Even worse, however, I got acquainted with the splendid achievements in the exploration of the ancient Near Eastern civilizations conducted by members of the University of Chicago Oriental Institute. The background thus had expanded to the ancient Near Eastern empires from whom Israel emerged, the Israelites were the background for the Christians, and the Christians were the background for the ideas of the Middle Ages. The pattern of a unilinear development of political ideas, from a supposed constitutionalism of Plato and Aristotle, through a dubious constitutionalism of the Middle Ages, into the splendid constitutionalism of the modern period, broke down.

The pattern, then, cracked along other lines. I had written my *History of Political Ideas* up well into the nineteenth century. Large chapters on Schelling, Bakunin, Marx, and Nietzsche were finished. While working on the chapter on Schelling, it dawned on me that the conception of a history of ideas was an ideological deformation of reality. There were no ideas unless there were symbols of immediate *experiences*. Moreover, one could not handle under the title of "ideas" an Egyptian coronation ritual, or the recitation of the *enuma Elish* on occasion of Sumerian New Year festivals. I was not yet in a position really to understand where the concept of ideas had come from and what it meant. Only very much later did I discover that the origin is probably to be found in the Stoic *koinai ennoiai*. These common, or self-evident, opinions were the starting point of criticism in chapter I of Locke's *Essay Concerning Human Understanding* (1690)—he protested against them in order to return to the experiences that engendered ideas.

These various occasions for becoming aware of the theoretical inadequacy of my conventional preconceptions about a history of ideas did not arise all at once and did not find immediate solutions. I would characterize the five years between 1945 and 1950 as a period of indecision, if not paralysis, in handling the problems that I saw but could not intellectually penetrate to my satisfaction. The work did not stop. I had to go on exploring sources, and the horizon grew even larger during the war, because China had become fashionable and the department decided that I, with my linguistic facility, would be elected to teach Chinese government. That threw me into the study of Chinese history; and because it was a bit difficult to talk about contemporary Chinese ideas without understanding their classical background, I started learning Chinese and learned enough to understand the symbols of the Classics, especially of Confucius and Lao-tse. This knowledge helped considerably in understanding Chinese thought. It is still helpful today, because I can recognize in the revolutionary operas propagated by Madame Mao Tse-tung the pattern of the ballet libretti of the Chou period, with the slight difference that the Chou authors celebrated the victory of the Chou Dynasty, whereas the modern revolutionary operas celebrate the victory of the revolutionary armies. Still, on the whole it was a period of theoretical paralysis with mounting problems for which I saw no immediate solutions.

A breakthrough occurred on occasion of the Walgreen Lectures that I delivered in Chicago in 1951. Here I was forced, in comparatively brief form, to formulate some of the ideas that had begun to crystallize. I concentrated on the problem of representation and the relation of representation to social and personal existence in truth. It was obvious that a Soviet government, for instance, was not in power by virtue of representative elections in the Western sense and nevertheless was the representative of the Russian people—but by virtue of what? This question I called at the time the problem of existential representation. This existential representation I found to be always the core of effective government, independent of the formal procedures by which the existentially representative government achieved its position. In a comparatively primitive society where the mass of the people is incapable of rational debate and of forming political parties who select issues, a government will rest on traditional or revolutionary forces without benefit of elections. That the government is tolerated is the result of its fulfilling more or less adequately the fundamental purposes for which any government is established—the securing of domestic peace, the defense of the realm, the administration of justice, and taking care of the welfare of the people. If these functions are fulfilled moderately well, the procedures by which the government comes into power are of secondary importance. This existential representation, then, I found empirically supplemented in historically existing societies by a claim to "transcendental" representation, as I called it at the time. By transcendental representation I meant the symbolization of the governmental function as representative of divine order in the cosmos. That is the fundamental symbolism, going back to the ancient Near Eastern empires where the king was the representative of the people before the god and of the god before the people. Nothing has changed in this fundamental structure of governmental order, not even in the modern ideological empires. The only difference is that the god whom the government represents has been replaced by an ideology of history that now the government represents in its revolutionary capacity.

The difference just mentioned had to be expressed in theoretical categories. For several years I had been aware, through my studies in the history of Christianity and the Middle Ages, of various sectarian movements not too clearly described with regard to their attitudes and beliefs. During the 1940s and 1950s, I became gradually aware that besides Classic philosophy and revelatory Christianity, as represented by the main church, there existed symbolizations of fundamental creeds that were classified as gnostic by experts in the field. So far as I remember, I became aware of the problem of Gnosticism and its application to modern ideological phenomena for the first time through the introduction of Hans Urs von Balthasar's *Prometheus*, published in 1937. Ever since the 1930s a considerable literature on Gnosticism had been growing, and incidental remarks concerning modern parallelisms were to be found here and there. I discovered that the continuity of Gnosticism from antiquity into the modern period was a matter of common knowledge among the better scholars of the eighteenth and the early nineteenth century. I should like to mention the great work by Ferdinand Christian Baur on *Die christliche Gnosis; oder, die christliche Religionsphilosophie in ihrer geschichtlichen Entwicklung* of 1835. Baur unfolded the history of Gnosticism from the original Gnosis of antiquity, through the Middle Ages, right into the philosophy of religion of Jakob Böhme, Schelling, Schleiermacher, and Hegel.

I want to stress that Gnosticism, as well as its history from antiquity to the present, is the subject of a vastly developed science, and that the idea of interpreting contemporary phenomena as gnostic is not as original as it may look to the ignoramuses who have criticized me for it. Generally I should like to remark that if I had discovered for myself all the historical and philosophical problems for which I am criticized by intellectuals, I would be without a doubt the greatest philosopher in the history of mankind. Before publishing anything on the applicability of gnostic categories to modern ideologies, I consulted with our contemporary authorities on Gnosticism, especially with Henri Charles Puech in Paris and Gilles Quispel in Utrecht. Puech considered it a matter of course that modern ideologies are gnostic speculations; and Quispel brought the Gnosticism of Jung, in which he was especially interested, to my attention.

Since my first applications of Gnosticism to modern phenomena in *The New Science of Politics* and in 1959 in my study on *Science, Politics, and Gnosticism*, I have had to revise my position. The application of the category of Gnosticism to modern ideologies, of course, stands. In a more complete analysis, however, there are other factors to be considered in addition. One of these factors is the metastatic apocalypse deriving directly from the Israelite prophets, via Paul, and forming a permanent strand in Christian sectarian movements right up to the Renaissance. An excellent exposition of this continuity is found in Norman Cohn's *The Pursuit of the Millennium*. I found, furthermore, that neither the apocalyptic nor the gnostic strand completely accounts for the process of immanentization. This factor has independent origins in the revival of neo-Platonism in Florence in the late fifteenth century. The attempt to regain an understanding of cosmic order through a revival of neo-Platonism miscarried; a revival of the divine order in the cosmos in the ancient sense would have required a revival of the pagan gods, and that did not work. What was left of the intracosmic divine order that the neo-Platonists tried to revive was an immanent order of reality—an immanentism that had to become secularist when, as today, following the pagan gods, the Christian God has been thrown out, too.

Hence, the *experiences* that result in immanentist constructions had to be explored. As historical phenomena, they are not unknown. Perhaps the most important one is the removal of the *amor Dei* from the Augustinian structure of the soul by Hobbes, and the reduction of its ordering force to the *amor sui*. This reduction to the *amor sui* then became dominant in the eighteenth century through the psychology of the *amour-de-soi* developed by the French *moralistes*. Although there is no doubt about the phenomenon as such, its interpretation is difficult because the conventional philosophical terminology has accepted the premises of the new reductionist position—that the position is reductionist does not come to analytical and critical attention. Only in recent years have I developed the concept of the "egophanic revolt," in order to designate the concentration on the epiphany of the ego as the fundamental experience that eclipses the epiphany of God in the structure of Classic and Christian consciousness. I had already used the term *apocalypse of man* to cover this problem in *The New Science of Politics*. On that occasion I wanted to stress the discovery of human possibilities that characterizes the modern period. No doubt this discovery was made, but stressing the discovery alone would not take into account its reductionist context. The discovery of man had to be paid for by the death of God, as this phenomenon was called by Hegel and Nietzsche. The term *egophanic revolt*, distinguishing this experience of the exuberant ego from the experience of the theophanic constitution of humanity, is the best I can do terminologically at present.

The term *metastatic apocalypse* will require a little explanation. I had to develop the term on occasion of the study of the Israelite prophets. In the prophecy of Isaiah we run into the oddity that Isaiah counseled the King of Judah not to rely on the fortifications of Jerusalem and the strength of his army but on his faith in Yahweh. If the king would have true faith, God would do the rest by producing an epidemic or a panic among the enemy, and the danger to the city would dissolve. The king had common sense enough not to follow the advice of the prophet but rather to rely on fortifications and military equipment. Still, there was the prophet's assumption that through an act of faith the structure of reality could be effectively changed.

In studying this problem and trying to understand it, my first idea, of course, was that the prophet indulged in magic, or at least believed in magic. That would not have been surprising, because in the history of Israel it had been the function of prophets, for instance, to guide the hand of the king in shooting a bow against the enemy as a magical operation that would result in victory. What happened in the case of Isaiah would have been what in modern psychology, by Nietzsche or Freud, would be called a sublimation of the more primitive physical magic. Still, I felt uneasy about it, and I consulted about the matter especially with Gerhard von Rad in Heidelberg, who was horrified at the idea that a grandiose spiritual prophet like Isaiah should be a magician. I was so impressed by his attitude that I made a concession. I did not use the term *magic* for the practice advised by Isaiah but coined a new term to characterize the peculiar sublimated magic belief in a transfiguration of reality through an act of faith. And this kind of faith I called *metastatic faith*—the belief in a metastasis of reality through an act of faith. I am not so sure that today I would make this concession, because this kind of faith is indeed magic, though one has to distinguish this "sublimated" variety from a more primitive magical operation. If one would really draw a hard line of difference between magic and metastatic faith, I am afraid the factor they have in common—the attempt to produce a desired result by means outside of the cause-effect relations in nature—would be smudged.

18

Alfred Schütz and the Theory of Consciousness

An important development in my understanding of the problems that worried me throughout the 1940s and well into the writing of *Order and History* was marked by my correspondence with Alfred Schütz on the problems of consciousness. They were not published until 1966 as the first part of my volume on *Anamnesis*. The correspondence with Schütz was precipitated by reading Edmund Husserl's *Krisis der europäischen Wissenschaften*. Husserl's study interested me greatly because of its magnificent sweep of history from Descartes to his own work. It also irritated me considerably because of the somewhat naïve arrogance of a philosopher who believed that his method of phenomenology had at last opened what he called the apodictic horizon of philosophy and that from now on everybody who wanted to be a solid philosopher had to be a follower of Husserl. This arrogance reminded me a bit too strongly of various other final philosophies like those of Hegel or Marx, and also of the conviction of National Socialists that theirs was the ultimate truth. I was especially disgusted by Husserl's language presumption in speaking of himself as the functionary of the spirit, because such language reminded me of recent experiences with functionaries of another sort. In continuation of my earlier analysis of consciousness in *Über die Form des amerikanischen Geistes*, I now went into an elaborative criticism of Husserl's conception of consciousness, the decisive point being that his model of consciousness was the sense perception of objects in the external world. While one could agree to the sophistication of analysis that he brought to bear on this model of perception, it seemed to me ridiculous to pretend that there was nothing to consciousness but the consciousness of objects of the external world. By that time, in 1942, I already knew enough about Classic, Patristic, and Scholastic philosophy to be aware that the philosophers who had founded philosophy on an analysis of consciousness were analyzing a few phenomena of consciousness besides the perception of objects in the external world. I went, therefore, into the question of what really were the experiences that form a man's consciousness; and I did that by an *anamnesis*, a recollection of decisive experiences of my childhood. As a matter of fact, I wrote twenty brief sketches, each giving such an early experience, so that they added up to something like an intellectual autobiography up to the age of ten.

The phenomena described were definitely phenomena of consciousness because they described my consciousness of various areas of reality as a child. And these experiences had very little to do with objects of sense perception. For instance, one of the experiences that had stuck firmly enough to be recollected forty years later was the story of the Monk of Heisterbach. Heisterbach was the ruin of a medieval monastery in the neighborhood of Königswinter where we frequently went for a Sunday excursion. The Monk of Heisterbach was a mythical monk who got lost, only to return after a thousand years and discover that these thousand years had passed for him like a single day. Such time concentrations and shortening, though obviously not problems of sense perception, constitute very relevant parts at least of my consciousness, even if they don't of Husserl's. In this manner, I went through such experiences as the anxieties and fascinations aroused by standing on the border of the known world with Hans Christian Andersen in one of his fairytales and looking north into a mysterious horizon of infinity, or experiences of festival movements in the life of man that I felt when I watched passing steamers on the Rhine with their night parties, and so forth. These types of experience constitute consciousness; and this is the *real* consciousness a man has, unless somebody wants to insist that my childhood was entirely different from that of any other child in the history of mankind. These experiences of participation in various areas of reality constitute the horizon of existence in the world. The stress lies on experiences of reality in the plural, being open to all of them and keeping them in balance. This is what I understood as the philosopher's attitude, and this is the attitude I found in the open existence of all great philosophers who by that time had come to my attention. To restore this openness of reality appeared to me to be the principal task of philosophy.

The analysis of experiences required a technical vocabulary. Fortunately I did not have to develop it from scratch but gradually to learn it from other philosophers who had gone through the same process and already found the terms by which they could signify the analytical steps in the exploration of their experiences. The center of consciousness I found to be the experience of participation, meaning thereby the reality of being in contact with reality outside myself. This awareness of participation as the central problem was fortified by the analysis of myth conducted by the members of the Chicago Oriental Institute under the category of consubstantiality, developed by the Frankforts and probably taken over from Levy-Bruhl. If man were not consubstantial with the reality that he experiences, he could not experience it. Among the philosophers, I found important confirmation from the Radical Empiricism of William James. James's study on the question, "Does 'Consciousness' Exist?" (1904), struck me at the time, and still strikes me, as one of the most important philosophical documents of the twentieth century. In developing his concept of pure experience, James put his finger on the reality of the consciousness of participation, inasmuch as what he calls *pure experience* is the something that can be put into the context either of the subject's stream of consciousness or of objects in the external world. This fundamental insight of James identifies the something that lies between the subject and object of participation as the experience. Later I found that the same type of analysis had been conducted on a much vaster scale by Plato, resulting in his concept of the *metaxy*—the In-Between. The experience is neither in the subject nor in the world of objects but In-Between, and that means In-Between the poles of man and of the reality that he experiences.

The In-Between character of experience becomes of particular importance for the understanding of response to the movements of divine presence. For the experience of such movements is precisely not located in man's stream of consciousness—man understood in the immanentist sense—but in the In-Between of the divine and the human. The experience is the reality of both divine and human presence, and only after it has happened can it be allocated either to man's consciousness or to the context of divinity under the name of revelation. A good number of problems that plague the history of philosophy now became clear as hypostases of the poles of a pure experience in the sense of William James, or of the *metaxy* experiences in the sense of Plato. By *hypostases* I mean the fallacious assumption that the poles of the participatory experience are self-contained entities that form a mysterious contact on occasion of an experience. A mystery, to be sure, is there, but even a mystery can be clearly expressed by stressing the participatory reality of the experience as the *site* of consciousness and understanding the *poles* of the experience as its poles and not as self-contained entities. The problem of reality experienced thus becomes the problem of a flow of participatory reality in which reality becomes luminous to itself in the case of human consciousness. The term *consciousness*, therefore, could no longer mean to me a human consciousness that is conscious of a reality outside man's consciousness, but had to mean the In-Between reality of the participatory pure experience that then analytically can be characterized through such terms as the poles of the experiential tension, and the reality of the experiential tension in the *metaxy*. The term *luminosity of consciousness*, which I am increasingly using, tries to stress this In-Between character of the experience as against the immanentizing language of a human consciousness, which, as a subject, is opposed to an object of experience.

This understanding of the In-Between character of consciousness, as well as of its luminosity—which is the luminosity not of a subjective consciousness but of the reality that enters into the experience from both sides—results further-more in a better understanding of the problem of symbols: *symbols* are the language phenomena engendered by the pro-cess of participatory experience. The language symbols ex-pressing an experience are not inventions of an immanentist human consciousness but are engendered in the process of participation itself. Language, therefore, participates in the *metaxy* character of consciousness. A symbol is neither a hu-man conventional sign signifying a reality outside conscious-ness nor is it, as in certain theological constructions, a word of God conveniently transmitted in the language that the recip-ient can understand; rather, it is engendered by the divine-human encounter and participates, therefore, as much in di-vine as in human reality. This seems to me, for the moment at least, the best formulation of the problem that plagues various symbolist philosophers—the problem that symbols do not simply signify a divine reality beyond consciousness but are somehow the divine reality in its presence itself. But I am afraid I have not yet completely worked out the details of this participatory philosophy of symbolism.

19

Order and Disorder

Frequently questions are raised concerning the meaning of *order* and *disorder* in my analysis. The reality of order is not my discovery. I am speaking of the order in reality discovered by mankind as far back as we have any written records, and now even farther back as we become familiar with the symbols in monuments discovered by archeologists as far back as the Paleolithicum. By *order* is meant the structure of reality as experienced as well as the attunement of man to an order that is not of his making—*i.e.*, the cosmic order. These insights into the structure and into the problem of adjustment or attunement, as I said, are present in literary documents as far back as the Egyptian third millennium B.C. To the same Egyptian millennium B.C. go back the literary expressions of experience of disorder, as in the development of radical skepticism regarding cosmic order when the daily experience was that of murderous disorder in the streets—as for instance in the famous *Dialogue of a Suicide with His Soul*, which I analyzed in my study on "Immortality: Experience and Symbol" (1967). In such experiences of social and cosmic disorder, order is reduced to one's own person and is perhaps not to be found even there; these experiences produce certain extreme states of alienation in which death may appear as the release from a prison or as convalescence from the mortal disease of life. Practically nothing has changed in these fundamental symbolisms of alienation since the third millennium B.C.

The categorization of these experiences of disorder, however, occurred fairly late. The concept of alienation (*allotri-*

osis), so far as I know, was first created by the Stoics and later
extensively used by Plotinus. In the Stoic psychopathology,
allotriosis means a state of withdrawal from one's own self as
constituted by the tension toward the divine ground of existence. Since the divine ground of existence is in Classic as well
as in Stoic philosophy the *logos* or the source of order in this
world, the withdrawal from one's self as constituted by this
ordering force is a withdrawal from reason in existence. The
result will then be the use of reason, which man has after all,
for the purpose of justifying existence in the state of alienation.
This far even the Stoics had advanced the psychopathology of
alienation.

The Stoic categories can be applied to modern ideological
phenomena in which the state of alienation, rather than the
state of existence in tension toward the divine ground, is used
as the experiential basis for an understanding of reality. The
systems of thinkers like Hegel are systematizations of a state
of alienation; inevitably they must arrive at the death of God,
not because God is dead but because divine reason has been
rejected in the egophanic revolt. One cannot revolt against
God without revolting against reason and vice versa. These
interpretations of reality on the basis of a deformed existence
that is no longer open to the reality of the ground, and has
therefore to remove the experience of the ground from any
consideration of reality, result in typical phenomena.

The most important such phenomenon is of course the
construction of *systems*. The system is a distinctly modern
phenomenon, though its modernity has been obscured by a
climate of opinion in which the system as the mode of philosophical thinking is taken so thoroughly for granted that the
reality of nonsystematic philosophizing has been eclipsed.
One speaks flatly, without thinking, of a Platonic or Aristotelian system, or of a Thomasic system, in spite of the fact that
these thinkers would have raised their hands in horror at the
idea that their empirical exploration of reality could ever result in a system. If anything was ever clear to a thinker like
Plato, who knew to distinguish between the experiences of
being and of not-being and acknowledged them both, it was

that for better or for worse reality was not a system. If therefore one constructs a system, inevitably one has to falsify reality. One of the important objects of inquiry concerning modern politics would have to be an inventory of the phenomena of systematic falsification, because they are a highly important factor of disorder in the contemporary situation. But the resistance to such inquiries is of course formidable, because precisely the persons who should engage in them are, as a group, the ones who would first have to discard their own systematic thought as a falsification of reality. And that, of course, they are not inclined to do. Still, the pressure of expanding historical knowledge, both with regard to political history and to the history of intellectual and spiritual phenomena, is increasing so strongly that one can reasonably predict (barring major social catastrophes that would bring a totalitarian systematizing sect to power) that the days of the systematizers and their disordering falsification of reality are numbered.

20

The Background of *Order and History*

My *History of Political Ideas* started from the conventional assumptions that there are ideas, that they have a history, and that a history of political ideas would have to work its way from Classical politics up to the present. Under these assumptions, I humbly worked through the sources, and eventually a manuscript of several thousand pages was in existence.

Still, the various misgivings that had arisen in the course of the work now crystallized into my understanding that a history of political ideas was a senseless undertaking, incompatible with the present state of science. Ideas turned out to be a secondary conceptual development, beginning with the Stoics, intensified in the high Middle Ages, and radically unfolding since the eighteenth century. Ideas transform symbols, which express experiences, into concepts—which are assumed to refer to a reality other than the reality experienced. And this reality other than the reality experienced does not exist. Hence, ideas are liable to deform the truth of the experiences and their symbolization.

The points at which misgivings had to arise are obvious. In the first place, there is no continuity between the so-called ideas of the Greek philosophers from the seventh to the fourth century B.C. and the contents of Israelite prophetic and New Testament revelatory writings. These two symbolizations touch different areas of experience and are not historically connected. Moreover, the farther one traces back the conventional origin of ideas, the more it becomes clear that such symbolisms as myth and revelation can by no stretch of the imagination be classified as "ideas." One must acknowledge a plurality of symbolisms. A Hesiodian theogony, for instance, is simply not a philosophy in the Aristotelian sense, even though the structure of reality expressed by myth and philosophy is the same—a sameness of structure already recognized by Aristotle. Problems were arising that I tried to express through such concepts as *compact,* or *primary experience of the cosmos,* and the *differentiations* that lead to the truth of existence in the Hellenic Classic, the Israelite, and the early Christian sense. In order to characterize the decisive transition from compact to differentiated truth in the history of consciousness, I used, at the time, the term *leap in being,* taking the term *leap* from Kierkegaard's *Sprung.*

The focus of my interest thus moved from ideas to the experiences of reality that engendered a variety of symbols for their articulation. That is not to say that the problem of ideas now simply disappeared. Of course it was very much present, but I only gradually found out what it was. An important point, for instance, which grew in clarity over the years, was the understanding that the transformation of original experiences-symbolizations into doctrines entailed a deformation of existence, if the contact with the reality as experienced was lost and the use of the language symbols engendered by the original experiences degenerated into a more or less empty game. Some of the most obvious things about this deformation I discovered rather late, only in the 1950s and 1960s. I had not been clearly aware, for instance, that the term *metaphysics* is not a Greek term but an Arabic deformation of the Greek title of Aristotle's *meta ta physica;* that it had been taken over from the Arabs by Thomas and used for the first time in a Western language in the introduction to his *Commentary* on Aristotle's *Metaphysics;* and that ever since there existed an odd science that was called metaphysics. Hence, the not-quite unjustified criticism of such doctrinal metaphysics by the thinkers of the Enlightenment and early Positivism did not touch the problems of Classic philosophy at all. Classic philosophy was not too well known at the time; and it is still little known today, because the cliché *metaphysics* has become the magic word by which one can cast a shadow on all philosophical analysis in the classic sense.

I had to give up "ideas" as objects of a history and establish the experience of reality—personal, social, historical, cosmic —as the reality to be explored historically. These experiences, however, one could explore only by exploring their articulation through symbols. The identification of the subject-matter and, with the subject-matter, of the method to be used in its exploration led to the principle that lies at the basis of all my later work: *the reality of experience is self-interpretive.* The men who have the experiences express them through symbols, and symbols are the key to understanding the experiences expressed. There is no sense in pretending that the Egyptian priests, for instance, who wrote the *Theology of Memphis* or the Mesopotamian priests who developed the *Sumerian King-List* were not able to articulate experiences clearly because they had other problems than a Voltaire, or a Comte, or a Hegel. What is experienced and symbolized as reality, in an advancing process of differentiation, is the substance of history. My work on the *History of Political Ideas* had not been done in vain, because it had familiarized me with the historical sources. But now the reorganization of the materials under the aspect of experience and symbolization became necessary. Hence, I gave up the project of a *History of Political Ideas* and started my own work on *Order and History*.

At the time, it seemed to me that *Order and History* had to begin with the Mesopotamian and Egyptian empires and their cosmological symbolization of personal and social order. Against this background of cosmological, imperial symbolism occurred the breakthrough of Israelite revelation. Not in continuity with the pneumatic prophets but independently, there occurred the outburst of noetic thinking in the Greek philosophers. The study of the Near Eastern and Israelite experiences down to the period of Christ filled the first volume of *Order and History*, and the evolution of the corresponding Greek experiences from the cosmological origins to the noetic differentiation filled volumes 2 and 3. According to the original plan, these volumes were to have been followed by studies on empire, medieval imperialism and spiritualism, and the modern development.

That plan, however, proved unrealizable. Considerable parts of it were in fact written, but the work broke down on the question of volume. I always ran into the problem that, in order to arrive at theoretical formulations, I had first to present the materials on which the theoretical formulations were based as an analytical result. If I went through with the program, the sequel to the first three volumes would have been not another three volumes as planned but perhaps six or seven volumes more. The general public was unfamiliar with the sources that led to certain theoretical insights, so the theoretical insights could not be presented without the sources.

I decided, therefore, to make a number of special studies on certain problems of early Christianity; the mytho-speculative form of historiogenesis; the transition from historiogenetic speculation to historiography; the problem of the ecumene as developed by Herodotus, Polybius, and the Chinese historians; certain modern theoretical problems, such as the sorcery involved in Hegel's construction of his system; and so forth. It seemed to make better sense to publish two volumes with these special studies, arriving more quickly at the theoretical results, than to fill numerous volumes with discussions of sources, especially since over the years what I had seen in the 1940s and 1950s as a problem had also been seen by others, and the historical exploration of such problems as Gnosticism, the Dead Sea scrolls, the Nag Hammadi finds, the prehistory of Pseudo-Dionysius, the revival of neo-Platonism in the Renaissance and its influences on subsequent intellectual Western developments up to Hegel, had made enormous progress, so that now I could refer to the studies of the sources conducted by a great number of scholars—sources that had not been accessible to the public in the 1940s and 1950s when I first developed the conception of *Order and History*. I want to stress the development just mentioned, because it could not be foreseen at the time I started my work. We are living today in a period of progress in the historical and philosophical sciences that hardly has a parallel in the history of mankind.

As a matter of fact, a number of the theoretical assumptions from which I started when I began to write *Order and History* have become obsolete through this rapid development of the historical sciences, especially in the fields of prehistory and archeology. When I wrote the first volume of *Order and History*, my horizon was still limited by the Near Eastern empires. I identified the cosmological symbolism that I found there with the imperial symbolism of Mesopotamia and Egypt. On the basis of the new expansion of our prehistoric and archeological knowledge, I can now say that practically all of the symbols that appear in the ancient Near East have a prehistory reaching through the Neolithicum back into the Paleolithicum, for a period of some twenty thousand years before the Near Eastern empires. There has arisen the new problem of disengaging the general problem of cosmological symbolism from its specific, imperial variation; the cosmological symbolisms on the tribal level, back to the Stone Age, must be analyzed; and then the *differentia specifica*, introduced by the foundation of empires, as for instance in Egypt, must be distinguished. I have collected the materials for this purpose; and I hope to publish my findings sometime in the future.

Another great advance in science that had been in the making for many decades has more recently found its decisive support through the recalibration of radiocarbon dates, beginning in 1966. The conception of a unilinear history, which had already been quite shaky in view of the chronologically parallel developments in the Near East, China, India, and Hellas, now definitely breaks down when the temple cultures in Malta, for instance, can be dated substantial periods of time before the Pyramid Age in Egypt. Independent neolithic civilizations precede in time the imperial civilizations in the Mesopotamian and Egyptian areas. Findings of this nature are accumulating in such quantities that one can say definitely even now that the older conception of a unilinear history, which still dominates the vulgarian level in the form of epigonal constructions in the wake of Condorcet, Comte, Hegel, and Marx, is definitely obsolete. The history of mankind has become diversified, because the differentiating developments were so widely dispersed. The field can be characterized as pluralistic. The progress, or general advance, of an imaginary abstract "mankind" has dissolved into the manifold of differentiating acts occurring at various points in time and independently in concrete human beings and societies.

The possibility of civilizational advance through cultural diffusion has not been excluded by these new aspects of history, but the problem must be pushed back to a much earlier period. As Carl Hentze once said to me in a conversation, if the history of articulate expression of experiences goes back for fifty thousand years, anything can have happened in that time; what can be found by way of cultural parallels in the so-called historical period after 3000 B.C. must be seen against the vast background of human social contacts in such time spans. To give an example: we have by now an excellent literature on Polynesian cultures, their art, and their myth. What is sometimes not realized is the fact that the Polynesians did not spring from the earth on the Polynesian islands but migrated there from the Asiatic mainland. This migration hardly began before the eighth century B.C. Hence, before that time the tribal developments that today we call Polynesian and other tribal developments that resulted in the rise of Chinese civilization belonged to the same area of culture. It is not surprising, therefore—as again Hentze observes—that there are highly interesting parallels between ornaments of Polynesian origin and ornaments on the vases of the Shang Dynasty.

The splendid advance of science in our time should not, however, induce rash expectations regarding the death of ideologies and their social effectiveness. The discrepancies between science and ideology are of long standing. As a matter of fact, certain ideological tenets were developed in flat contradiction to ordinary historical facts well known at the time and especially to the ideological thinkers. When Marx and Engels, for instance, begin their *Communist Manifesto* with the proposition that all social history hitherto has been the history of class struggle, they are talking impertinent nonsense, because there were, after all, other struggles in history, well known to Marx and Engels from their high school days, such as the Persian Wars, the conquests of Alexander, the Peloponnesian War, the Punic Wars, and the expansion of the Roman Empire, which had definitely nothing to do with class struggles. If ideologists can make such propagandistic nonsense statements and get away with them for more than a century, one should not expect the expansion of our historical knowledge through science to make a dent in the corrupt existence of the ideological epigone in our own time. These last remarks, however, should not be understood as expressing a profound pessimism. That happens to be an eighteenth-century mood and is today somewhat anachronistic.

21

Teaching Career

In addition to the actual work in science in which I try to participate as far as my powers permit, I have for fifty years functioned as a teacher. My teaching experience started in high school. Since we were poor, I had to get some minimum pocket money by way of tutoring other high school students who were the children of more affluent parents but did not match their material affluence with intelligence and industriousness. This kind of work continued until I finished high school. When I started work at the university, I had the good luck of getting a job as a volunteer assistant in the Handels-vereinigung-Ost, an Austrian-Ukrainian enterprise that had grown out of the occupation of the Ukraine by the Central European powers during World War I. One of the students whom I had tutored was the son of the secretary general of the Chamber of Commerce in Vienna, who saw to it that I got this job, which, though very low paying, enabled me to continue my studies. Very soon after I got acquainted with the professors at the university in seminars, there opened up the possibility of a teaching position, with a very, very small salary, at the Volkshochschule Wien-Volksheim. This institution was an adult education project sponsored by the Socialist government of the city of Vienna, where the students were the intellectually more alert and industrious radicals from the workers' environment. I must stress the "intellectually more alert," because the less-alert stratum of workers entering the political process was of course taken care of by the trade-union training courses. The Volkshochschule was something like a university for workers as well as lower-middle-class young people.

In this environment I learned to discuss and debate. At the time I accepted the job, I had already gone far beyond my three months of Marxism in the summer of 1919, and now I was facing these rather radical Socialists, most of them probably outright Communists. Since the subjects I had to teach were political science and the history of ideas, wild debates immediately ensued in which I could not give in or I would have lost my authority. During these years a permanent good relationship developed between the young radicals and myself, and I continued this kind of work after I came back from America and France in 1927, until I was removed by the National Socialists in 1938. Though the conflict between the young Marxists and my first attempts at being a scientifically oriented scholar was always strongly articulate, the personal relations were the best. After the lecture and seminar hours in the evening, after nine o'clock, the group always got together and continued the discussions in one of the numerous coffeehouses in the neighborhood. I still remember a scene in the 1930s when, after a wild debate resulting in disagreement, one of these young fellows, not so very much younger than I was myself, with tears in his eyes told me, "And when we come to power we have to kill you."

This little incident is perhaps the occasion for another story that characterizes the Austrian social climate. After the Social Democratic uprising in 1934, certain Social Democratic leaders were arrested and put in jail for a short while, not for very long. But one of them, the famous Max Adler, their chief ideologist, was not arrested. That was a horrible blow to his self-esteem, because now the government had attested what everybody knew—that he was politically an entirely unimportant figure. Friends of Max Adler, who after all was a colleague of mine in the Law Faculty, asked me on occasion whether I could not do something through my equally good relations with the other side to get him arrested for a little while, so that he would not be so terribly sad and downhearted. I actually talked with one of my colleagues, who was a high government official and was at the same time teaching administrative law at the university, and asked whether the government could not arrest Adler for at least the forty-eight hours permitted under the habeas corpus provisions before they had to release him. We talked about the matter, he was very obliging and courteous, he said that he understood Adler's situation perfectly well, and since he was also a colleague of his in the same faculty he would like to do what he could to accommodate him, but he was afraid no one could do anything. If Adler were arrested, the government would make itself ridiculous, because everybody knew that Max Adler was unimportant. He really could not oblige him.

My good relations with these young radicals lasted well into the Nazi period. They became even more intense in the 1930s because everybody knew that if I was not a Communist, I was still less a National Socialist. When the blow of the occupation fell, I was able to help some of these radicals with letters of recommendation for their flight to safer areas, like Sweden. At the University of Vienna, however, where I began to teach as a *Privatdozent* in 1929, relations with the students were fraught with tensions because these students came from middle-class homes, they were not workers, and the intellectually more active ones were to a considerable degree affected by the German nationalism rampant in that middle class, as well as by anti-Semitism. There were no open conflicts, but relations were not warm. In 1938, when the National Socialist occupation came, I observed that quite a number of the students whom the day before I had had in my seminar on administrative procedure donned the black uniform of the SS.

For a real experience with Central European students, as distinguished from young worker-radicals, I can speak only for the years of my professorship in Munich from 1958 to 1969. Because I had been called to Munich to organize a hitherto nonexistent Institute of Political Science, I had to acquire first of all a couple of assistants who would help in building up a library and taking care of the quite considerable number of students who flocked into the lecture courses and the seminars. From these beginnings, with a number of completely empty rooms that had to be filled with library shelves and books on the shelves, there developed the institute that lasted until I left in 1969. Gradually a body of students grew who themselves became an educative force for other students attracted to political science. The results of these eleven years must be described as a considerable success. In the first place, there was the institute as a physical establishment, with a first-rate library—a collection that covered new developments in the historical sciences, not only in German but above all in English and French. Special attention was given to the various areas that are basic for the understanding of Western culture—that is, to Classic philosophy, Judaism, and Christianity; the sections on modern history and modern political ideas had to be brought up to date as quickly as possible; and new developments in prehistory, in the ancient Near East, China, India, and Africa, as well as new archeological discoveries, had to be taken care of. The library became famous and was extensively used by young scholars from other fields because it was the best all-around library for developments in the contemporary sciences of man and society.

The young people also did well, and we began publishing monographs representing the work of the institute. The most important of these series is the *Schriftenreihe zur Politik und Geschichte*, published by the List Verlag in Munich, now running over ten volumes. Of the areas and problems covered, I mention the work by Peter Weber-Schaefer on the Chinese ecumene, by Peter J. Opitz on Lao-tse, and by Peter von Sivers on the political theories of Ibn-Khaldun. There were further studies dealing mostly with eighteenth- and nineteenth-century Western intellectual history, and monographs by Manfred Henningsen on Toynbee's *A Study of History*, by Michael Naumann on Karl Kraus, by Eckard Kolberg on LaSalle, by Hedda Herwig on Freud and Jung, by Tilo Schabert on the symbolisms of nature and revolution in the French eighteenth century, and by Dagmar Herwig on Robert Musil. To these years also belongs the work by Professor Ellis Sandoz on Dostoevsky, whose book (published in 1971) first came out as a Ph.D. dissertation in Munich. During the ten years, the

firstcomers in the institute grew older and became independent. Three of them—Peter J. Opitz, Manfred Henningsen, and
Jürgen Gebhardt—became the highly active editors of a paper-
back *Geschichte des politischen Denkens*, of which some
eleven volumes have come out by now. Peter Opitz has also
become the editor of a collected volume of essays on Chinese
revolution from the middle of the nineteenth century to the
Communist movement. Others who entered the institute
later from other fields have also produced interesting new
studies. I should like to mention Klaus Vondung and his
book on *Magie und Manipulation*. The older ones among the
younger people who started working with me are now themselves in professional positions, or near them, and the aggregate of the group and its work has become a distinct force on
the German intellectual scene—though I cannot say that this
particular group and its force are loved by the ideologists, left
or right.

I am frequently asked about my experiences regarding the
difference between European and American students. There
are marked differences but not of such a nature that I should
say that one type is preferable to the other. They have their
peculiarities. With the Germans, I found a very high degree of
background knowledge that facilitated their progress to independent work in science. The people whom I admitted to my
seminars, and especially the ones who became assistants and
conducted their own seminars, had a knowledge of at least one
Classical language and of course were able to read German,
French, and English fluently. Some of them had additional
knowledge of languages in their particular field. The Islamists,
for instance, had under the regulations of the university to
have a good knowledge of Arabic and Turkish; the students
dealing with Far Eastern affairs had to know Chinese and Jap-
anese in addition to the Western languages. That made for a
group of highly educated, intellectually alert young people
who certainly helped each other in the sharp contest of com-
petitive debate of problems. One of their favorite games, of
course, was to catch me out on some technical mistake, but
unfortunately I could offer them the pleasure only rarely.

The American students belonged to widely different types. In Louisiana there was a considerable cultural background provided by the Catholic parochial schools. I had students in my courses who knew Latin and who took courses in Thomist philosophy with the Catholic chaplain at Louisiana State University. That of course helped. The average students, I should say, did not have the background knowledge one would expect of European students, but they had instead something that the European, especially the German, students usually lack—a tradition of common-sense culture. In the South especially, the problem of ideological corruption among young people was negligible. The students were open-minded and had little contact with ideological sectarian movements. My experiences in the East were less favorable. The ideological corruption of the East Coast has affected the student mind profoundly, and occasionally these students betray the behavioral characteristics of totalitarian aggressiveness. A great number of students simply will not tolerate information that is not in agreement with their ideological prejudices. I frequently had difficulties with students of this type. Still, on the whole, even the so-called radical students, short of the hard-core militants, can be handled by swamping them with mountains of information. They still have enough common sense to be aware that their own ideas must bear some relation to the reality surrounding them; and when it is brought home to them that their picture of reality is badly distorted, they do not become easy converts but at least they begin to have second thoughts. I cannot say the same of radical students in Germany, who simply start shouting and rioting if any serious attempt is made to bring into discussion facts that are incompatible with their preconceptions.

During the years in Louisiana, my wife and I acquired our American citizenship. There was an amusing detail. The Department of Justice, in charge of immigration procedures, had issued a little book that formulated the principal questions that could be asked and the answers one had to give. I noticed that the Department of Justice, in spite of Roosevelt and the war, was still quite conservative—the American form of government was a *republic*; if you said it was a democracy you were wrong. I believe these questionnaire leaflets have by now been changed.

So far as my faculty position in Louisiana is concerned, I advanced from associate professor to full professor with tenure, and ultimately I became one of the first Boyd Professors, together with T. Harry Williams, when the university introduced these professorships in order to pay higher salaries to some scholars whose services they wanted to retain. Still, when in the second half of the 1950s I was offered the professorship in Munich, I did not refuse. There were several reasons. In the first place, I could organize my own institute and train young scholars who would continue the work that I had initiated. Second, at the time the salary in Munich was higher than the salary in Louisiana. Third, old friends like Alois Dempf, the historian and philosopher, had been highly instrumental in getting me to Munich, and I certainly had no objections to entering this very congenial intellectual and spiritual environment. Besides, the spirit of American democracy would be a good thing to have in Germany.

Under this last aspect, the beginnings were a bit difficult, because German students were not accustomed to speak up freely as American students do. Even those who became assistants had to be pushed very energetically into an attitude of personal independence that differed starkly from the very subordinate position in which assistants are kept in numerous cases by the old-style German professor. Not the least point of attraction the institute had for me was the group of young people who so signally differed in the behavior that I inculcated in them from the type of behavior preferred in other institutes in Munich. On the whole, however, I believe that the idea of injecting an element of international consciousness, and of democratic attitudes, into German political science has not been much of a success beyond the immediate circle of young people that I could train personally. As I later analyzed the situation in my lecture on the German university [1966; English, 1985], the damage of National Socialism has been enormous. What one might call the universitarian upper stratum was simply killed off, partly through actual murder, so that the type of professors whom I met in 1929 in Heidelberg simply disappeared without leaving a younger generation trained by them. However, the universitarian middle and lower class survived in force; they now determine the general climate of the German universities, and that climate is mediocre and limited. The aftereffects of National Socialism make themselves felt in the contemporary destruction of the German university through an invasion of the rabble from below to which the university personnel cannot offer any effective resistance because the authority of the great scholars in the universities disappeared with the scholars themselves. The general prospects, therefore, I consider very dubious.

When I say the prospects are dubious, I mean that in fact the active operation of the universities, especially in the fields of the social sciences and the humanities, has been widely destroyed through the famous democratization, especially through the participatory democracy, which means in fact that nobody is permitted to do his work in peace. In a case like Berlin, for instance, leftist students simply do not permit anybody who is not a Marxist to open his mouth; and I hear that a similar situation exists in places like Marburg. Munich was fortunately preserved from the worst effects, partly because my institute there was a stronghold of nonideological science. I should like to stress this point because people sometimes underrate the effect a professor can have, not by throwing his weight around but by educating in his courses and seminars two or three annual classes of students who then become an effective propaganda force against ideologists among the other students. That of course will wear off if an energetic attitude is not maintained, or if it is made ineffective by rapidly increasing the staff, so that the institute becomes dominated by mediocre people who cannot properly resist radical students in debate.

22

Why Philosophize? To Recapture Reality!

The motivations of my work, which culminates in a philosophy of history, are simple. They arise from the political situation. Anybody with an informed and reflective mind who lives in the twentieth century since the end of the First World War, as I did, finds himself hemmed in, if not oppressed, from all sides by a flood of ideological language—meaning thereby language symbols that pretend to be concepts but in fact are unanalyzed *topoi* or topics. Moreover, anybody who is exposed to this dominant climate of opinion has to cope with the problem that language is a social phenomenon. He cannot deal with the users of ideological language as partners in a discussion, but he has to make them the object of investigation. There is no community of language with the representatives of the dominant ideologies. Hence, the community of language that he himself wants to use in order to criticize the users of ideological language must first be discovered and, if necessary, established.

The peculiar situation just characterized is not the fate of the philosopher for the first time in history. More than once in history, language has been degraded and corrupted to such a degree that it no longer can be used for expressing the truth of existence. This was the situation, for instance, of Sir Francis Bacon when he wrote his *Novum Organum*. Bacon classified the unanalyzed topics current in his time as "idols": the idols of the cave, the idols of the marketplace, the idols of pseudo-theoretical speculation. In resistance to the dominance of idols—*i.e.*, of language symbols that have lost their contact with reality—one has to rediscover the experiences of reality as well as the language that will adequately express them. The situation today is not very different. One has only to remember Alexander Solzhenitsyn's chapter on "Idols of the Market-place" in *Cancer Ward* (chapter 31) in order to recognize the continuity of the problem. Solzhenitsyn had to fall back on Bacon and his conception of idols in order to defend the reality of Reason in his own existence against the impact of Communist dogma. I like to refer to the case of Solzhenitsyn because his awareness of the problem, as well as his competence as a philosopher in his reference to Bacon, is certainly a model that would, if followed, fundamentally change the intellectual climate of our universities and colleges. In relation to the dominant climate of the social sciences, the philosopher in America finds himself very much in the situation of Solzhenitsyn in relation to the Soviet Writer's Union—the important difference, of course, being that our Soviet Writer's Union cannot enlist governmental power for the purpose of suppressing scholars. Hence, there are always enclaves in the West in which science can continue, and even flourish, in spite of the intellectual terrorism of institutions such as the mass media, university departments, foundations, and commercial publishing houses.

A situation comparable to the present one occurred at the time when Plato started his work. In the conventional interpretation of Plato, it is practically forgotten that the central Platonic concepts are dichotomic. The term *philosophy* does not stand alone but gains its meaning from its opposition to the predominant philodoxy. Problems of justice are not developed in the abstract but in opposition to wrong conceptions of justice, which in fact reflect the injustice current in the environment. The character of the Philosopher himself gains its specific meaning through its opposition to that of the Sophist, who engages in misconstructions of reality for the purpose of gaining social ascendance and material profits.

This is the situation in which the philosopher has to find the men of his own kind in a community that comprehends both the present and the past. Although there is always a dominant climate of ideological opinion, there is also present, even in our society, a large community of scholars who have not lost contact with reality and of thinkers who try to regain the contact that they are in danger of losing. One of the typical phenomena of the twentieth century is the event of spiritually energetic people breaking out of the dominant intellectual group in order to find the reality that has been lost. Famous cases have been, for England, the breakout of George Orwell from his intellectual surroundings; in France, the breakout of Albert Camus from the Parisian intellectual environment; in Germany, the gigantic work of Thomas Mann in his effort to break out of the ideologies of the Wilhelminean period and the Weimar Republic, culminating in his great philosophy of history in the introduction to the Joseph novels.

The most important means of regaining contact with reality is the recourse to thinkers of the past who had not yet lost reality, or who were engaged in the effort of regaining it. The question of where to start is frequently one of biographical accident. A man like Camus had recourse to the myth that was biographically closest to him through his education and upbringing in North Africa. A similar recourse to myth, as well as to Israelite revelation, is found in the work of Thomas Mann. In this last case, one can also discern where contemporary support for the effort originates, as in the relation between Thomas Mann and Karl Kerényi. Generally speaking, the reservoirs of reality in our society are to be found in the sciences that deal with intact experiences and symbolizations of reality, even if the sciences themselves have been badly damaged by the influence of the ideological climate.

So far as my own experience is concerned, such areas are Classic philosophy and the works of students of Classic philosophy, such as Paul Friedländer, Werner Jäger, E. R. Dodds, or Bruno Snell. Another such area is Patristic and Scholastic philosophy, as well as the works of contemporary representatives such as Étienne Gilson and Henri de Lubac. A third area is the history of the ancient Near East. I have pointed to the influence I received from the Chicago Oriental Institute and from the vast advance of the study of ancient history during the last thirty years. A further area is comparative religion; I have mentioned the influences I received from students of Gnosticism, and generally of early comparative religion, like Mircea Eliade, Puech, and Quispel. More recently, there has been the study of early symbolisms, extending back to the Paleolithicum.

On occasion I have remarked on the odd social phenomenon that our universities are sprinkled with scholars for whom the exploration of Stone Age symbolisms, Neolithic civilizations, ancient civilizations, or the Classic Chinese or Hindu civilization, is the means of regaining a spiritual ground that they do not find on the dominant level of our universities and churches. The social problem just adumbrated is still far too little explored, but for its importance I can testify from my personal experience. As a student I was surrounded by the intellectual climate of neo-Kantian methodology. In the circle of the Pure Theory of Law in Vienna, a philosopher was a person who based his methodology on Kant; a historian was a person who read any books written before Kant. Hence, my interest in Classic philosophy, which was already marked at that time, was interpreted by my colleagues as historical interest and as an attempt to escape from the true philosophy represented by the neo-Kantian thinkers. This problem of reconstructing a society that includes as its members the great thinkers of the past inevitably brings to mind Machiavelli's famous letter in which he describes to his friend Francesco Vettori [December 10, 1513] the course of his days in lowly occupations in the dubious rural society of San Casciano, then how, when evening comes, he dons festival garb, goes to his study, and joins the company of the ancients for urbane intercourse and conversation.

Recapturing reality in opposition to its contemporary deformation requires a considerable amount of work. One has to reconstruct the fundamental categories of existence, experience, consciousness, and reality. One has at the same time to explore the technique and structure of the deformations that clutter up the daily routine; and one has to develop the concepts by which existential deformation and its symbolic expression can be categorized. This work, then, must be conducted not only in opposition to the deformed ideologies but also to deformations of reality by thinkers who ought to be its preservers, such as theologians.

In the concrete effort to find one's way through a maze of corrupt language toward reality and its adequate linguistic expression, certain rules emerge that are not always to the liking of our contemporary intellectuals. The methodologically first, and perhaps most important, rule of my work is to go back to the experiences that engender symbols. No language symbol today can be simply accepted as a bona fide symbol, because corruption has proceeded so far that everything is suspect. In the course of this effort, I found that I had to explore the meaning of *philosophy* as a symbol created by the Classic philosophers, its meaning to be determined on the basis of the text. Such changes of meaning as this symbol has suffered in the course of time then have to be determined with care by relating them to the original meaning, because only on the basis of such comparative studies can one judge whether the change of meaning is justified (because it takes into account aspects of reality that were not included in the original meaning) or whether the change of meaning is unjustified (because elements of reality have been excluded in order to construct a new, defective concept).

This rule of analytical inquiry frequently arouses the opposition of intellectuals, as I have experienced in discussions, because they insist on the right to give to words whatever meanings they want. The existence of a standard based on the historical fact that words do not lie around in a language, but are created by thinkers for the expression of experiences when they have them, is fervently rejected. They prefer what I call the Humpty-Dumpty philosophy of language: determining the meanings of words is an exercise of the intellectual's power that must not be submitted to criticism.

Considerable help in understanding the processes of deformation has come to me from the observation of these processes by the great Austrian novelists, especially Albert Paris Gütersloh, Robert Musil, and Heimito von Doderer. They coined the term *second reality* in order to signify the image of reality created by human beings when they exist in a state of alienation. The principal characteristic of this state of alienation, which is supported by the imaginative construction of second realities in opposition to the reality of experience, is what Doderer has called the "refusal to apperceive" (Apperzeptionsverweigerung). The concept appears in his novel *Die Dämonen*, and I always enjoy the fact that he developed it while discussing certain sexual aberrations. The concept of *Apperzeptionsverweigerung* is formally developed in the introductory remarks to the chapter on "Die dicken Damen"— fat ladies—who are preferred by one of his heroes.

The refusal to apperceive has become for me the central concept for the understanding of ideological aberrations and deformations. It appears in a variety of phenomena, of which the historically most interesting is the formal interdict on questioning demanded by Comte and Marx. If anybody should question their ideological doctrine by raising the question of the divine ground of reality, he will be informed by Comte that he should not ask idle questions ("questions oiseuses"), and by Marx that he should shut up and become a "socialist man" ("Denke nicht, frage mich nicht," Don't think, don't ask me).

This attitude of not permitting questions regarding their premises—questions that would immediately explode the system—is the general tactic employed by ideologists in discussion. In numerous conversations with Hegelians, for instance, I have always come to the point where I had to question the premises of alienated existence that lie at the basis of Hegel's speculation. Whenever this question comes up, I am informed by the respective Hegelian that I don't understand Hegel and that one can understand Hegel only if one accepts his premises without questioning them. If the interdict on questions is understood as the central tactic of all ideological debate, one has gained at least one important criterion for diagnosing an ideology: the purpose of the diagnosis is to determine which part of reality has been excluded in order to make the construction of a fake system possible. The realities excluded can vary widely, but the one item that always has to be excluded is the experi-

ence of man's tension toward the divine ground of his existence.

Once the consciousness of existential tension is recognized
as the critical experience that an ideologist must exclude if he
wants to make his own state of alienation compulsory for everybody, the problem of consciousness of this tension moves
into the center of philosophical thought. The understanding of
both Classic and Christian philosophy, as well as of ideological
deformations of existence, presupposes the understanding of
consciousness in the fullness of its dimensions. The characteristic of what may be called the "modern conception of consciousness" is the construction of consciousness by the model
of sense perceptions of objects in external reality. This restriction of the model of consciousness to objects of external reality
becomes the more or less hidden trick in the construction of
systems in the nineteenth century. Even in the core of Hegel
one can observe, in his *Phenomenology*, that he begins with
sense perception and from this basis develops all higher structures of consciousness. The case is remarkable because Hegel
was one of the greatest connoisseurs of the history of philosophy; he knew, of course, that the primary experiences of consciousness as they appear in the work of the Classic philosophers are not concerned with sense perceptions but with the
experience of structures (as, for instance, mathematical structures) and the experience of the turning toward the divine
ground of existence motivated by the pull exerted by this
ground. I have not the slightest doubt that a man with Hegel's
historical knowledge deliberately ignored the immediate experiences of consciousness and replaced them with the highly
abstract, and historically very late, models of perception of
objects in the external world, in order to put over a system that
expressed his state of alienation. I do not know of any passage
in Hegel where he reflects on his technique of intellectual
fraud, but the technique has become explicit in the work of
Marx, in the Paris Manuscripts of 1844.

If the experience of objects in the external world is abso-
lutized as the structure of consciousness at large, all spiritual

and intellectual phenomena connected with experiences of divine reality are automatically eclipsed. However, since they cannot be totally excluded—because after all they are the history of humanity—they must be deformed into propositions about a transcendental reality. This propositional deformation of the philosophers' and prophets' symbols is one of the important phenomena in the history of mankind. It is already highly developed in Scholastic philosophy, further hardened in the transition to modern metaphysics in Descartes, and then continued as a sort of secondary orthodoxy by the ideological thinkers. That propositional metaphysics is a deformation of philosophy, consistently continued in doctrinal ideology, I consider one of my more important findings.

Once this problem is recognized, the question arises of why human beings engage in games of propositional metaphysics, as well as in the successor orthodoxies of propositional ideologies. What is the experiential motive of the great modern dogmatomachies from the sixteenth century onward, now going on for more than four hundred years without a return to the predogmatic reality of experienced insight?

This question leads to the problem of alienation—*i.e.*, the state of existence that expresses itself in the deformation of symbols into doctrines. The problem is, of course, not new. The deformations began in Classic antiquity as soon as the myth of the *polis* became an empty shell through the destruction by the empires of the society that had engendered the symbolism. With the Stoics and their observation of existential disorder in the wake of imperial conquest begins the understanding of alienation, expressing itself in the creation of the term *allotriosis*. The Stoics, being well-trained philosophers themselves, understood the phenomenon of alienation quite well. If philosophical existence is existence in awareness of man's humanity as constituted by his tension toward the divine ground, and if this awareness is in the practice of existence realized by the Platonic *periagoge*—the turning toward the ground—then alienation is the turning away from the ground toward a self that is imagined to be human without being constituted by its relation to the divine presence. The turning toward the divine ground—the Classic *epistrophe*—is therefore to be supplemented in the description of states of human existence by the Stoic conception of *apostrophe*—the turning away from the ground. Turning toward, and turning away from, the ground become the fundamental categories descriptive of the states of order and disorder in human existence.

These fundamental observations of the Stoics concerning the structure of existence tie in with the previously mentioned modern observations on the refusal to apperceive. Turning away means to refuse to apperceive the experience of the divine ground as constitutive of man's reality. This willful turning away from the fundamental experience of reality was diagnosed by the Stoics as a disease of the mind. The science of existential deformation through turning away from the ground, and thereby withdrawing from one's own self, became the core of psychopathology and remained the core well into the Renaissance.

The issue has come to the fore again in the twentieth century, because the mass phenomena of spiritual and intellectual disorientation in our time have attracted attention again to the fundamental act of *apostrophe*. After finding the causes of disorder in a variety of secondary symptoms, like an undisciplined indulgence of the passions, one discovers now again, in existential psychology, that behind the secondary symptoms lies the fundamental problem of the *apostrophe*—the withdrawal of man from his own humanity.

The phenomenon of the rediscovery just described is not peculiar to the modern period. We can observe it in the Classic Greek period, when the observation of social pathology, couched by Thucydides in the medical terms of the Hippocratic school, became the basis for the discovery of existential order by Plato and Aristotle. In a very similar manner today, having gone through two centuries of severe distortion of existence, the phenomenon is beginning to be understood as pathological; and as it is being discovered as pathological, the question of sane, well-ordered existence again attracts attention.

23

Philosophy of History

These various developments affect the problems of a philosophy of history. Philosophy of history as a topic does not go farther back than the eighteenth century. From its beginning in the eighteenth century, it became associated with the constructions of an imaginary history made for the purpose of interpreting the constructor and his personal state of alienation as the climax of all preceding history. Until quite recently, philosophy of history has been definitely associated with the misconstruction of history from a position of alienation, whether it be in the case of Condorcet, Comte, Hegel, or Marx. This rigid construction of history as a huge falsification of reality from the position of an alienated existence is dissolving in the twentieth century. Once the deformation of existence, which leads to the construction of ideological systems, is recognized as such, the categories of undeformed human existence become the criteria by which deformed existence and systems must be judged. Hence, the ideological systems themselves become historical phenomena in a process that reflects, among other things, the human tension between order and disorder of existence. There are periods of order, followed by periods of disintegration, followed by the misconstruction of reality by disoriented human beings. Against such disintegration, disorientation, and misconception there arise the countermovements in which the fullness of reality is restored to consciousness.

In the light of this conception of order and disorder, one can interpret certain aspects of the so-called modernity as an expression of deformed existence in the same sense in which Thucydides, in his *History of the Peloponnesian War*, described the course of the war and its prehistory as a social *kinesis*—a feverish movement of disintegration and disorder. This does not mean, however, that at the time of such movements, be it the period under survey by Thucydides or the modern *kinesis* since the eighteenth century, feverish disorder alone dominates the scene. Although "modernity" in the pejorative sense is undeniably a characteristic of the modern period, there goes on, at the same time, the resistance to disorder, as well as the efforts to regain the reality lost or distorted. However one wishes to construct the concept of *modernity*, it will have to cover both the destruction of reality committed by alienated human beings (the ideological thinkers) for the purpose of their own aggrandizement, and the countermovement of philosophers and scholars, which in our time culminates in the splendid advance of the historical sciences, revealing as grotesque the ideological constructions that still dominate the scene. One can find today, on the one hand, a massive revisionist movement among American historians who rewrite the history of the Cold War with a Marxist bias and, on the other hand, the characterization of such activities as "para-Marxist buffoonery" by a scholar like Raymond Aron.

If the concepts of order and disorder of existence are applied to the ever-increasing amount of historical materials, certain structural lines of meaning begin to emerge—always with the reservation, of course, that they may have to be revised in the light of advancing historical knowledge. One of the important results that will be incorporated in the forthcoming volume 4 of *Order and History* [published in 1974] is the description of the Ecumenic Age. By *Ecumenic Age* is meant a period in the history of mankind extending roughly from the time of Zoroaster and the beginnings of the Achemenide conquest to the end of the Roman Empire. This is the period in which the cosmological understanding of reality was definitely replaced by a new understanding of reality, centered in the differentiation of the truth of existence through Hellenic philosophy and the Christian revelatory experiences. Geographically, the Ecumenic Age extends from the Persian, and in its wake the Greek and Roman, developments in the West to the parallel development of ecumenic consciousness in the Far Eastern civilizations, especially in China. One of the aspects of this age has been caught in the concept of the *Axis-time*, the period in which, around 500 B.C., Heraclitus, the Buddha, and Confucius were contemporaries. Another aspect of this Ecumenic Age is the phenomenon which has given it its name—*i.e.*, the imperial expansion through the Persians, Alexander, the Romans, the Maurya dynasty in India, and the Ch'in and Han dynasties in China. By about 200 B.C. we are no longer in a world of tribal societies or of small city states, but in the world of the ecumenic empires extending from the Atlantic to the Pacific. I have spoken of an ecumenic consciousness, meaning thereby that the actors and contemporaries of the imperial events interpreted them as a discovery and conquest of what they called the *ecumene*, as did Herodotus, or Polybius, or in China the first historians Ssu-ma T'an and Ssu-ma Ch'ien. The symbol *ecumene* becomes the *idée-force* of this period; and ecumenic conquest in the sense of domination over contemporarily living mankind has remained a fundamental force of history ever since, even if in practice the realization of such ecumenic—which now would have to become global—domination has never been achieved. The Ecumenic Age, therefore, has to be characterized by three of its more spectacular phenomena: (1) the spiritual outbursts on which Jaspers concentrated; (2) the imperial concupiscential outbursts that have always attracted the attention of historians; and (3) the beginnings of historiography, in which the disorder created by the destructive expansion of empire is weighed against the order established, and the order established is measured by the newly differentiated understanding of existential order.

This triadic structure of spiritual outburst, empire, and historiography characterizes a period in the history of mankind. In my opinion it has to supersede other constructions of history, even nonideological constructions, such as for instance Toynbee's earlier assumption of civilizations as the ultimate units of historical study. Civilizations can hardly be maintained as ultimate units in the face of the multicivilizational empires created by the Persians, the Greeks under Alexander, and the Romans, and of their disintegration into ethnic sub-units when the impetus of imperial expansion had run into various obstacles. Moreover, in order to arrive at the concept of civilization as the ultimate unit, Toynbee had to construct civilizational units in retrospect from the imperial establishments that he considered their last phase before a disintegrating interregnum. As a matter of fact, the "civilizations" that culminate in "ecumenic empires" did not exist before imperial expansion. There certainly is something like a continuity of Chinese history, say from the Classic Chou period into the Han and post-Han empire, but the Chinese civilization emerging from the imperial ordeal is definitely not the aggregate of tribal societies that entered into it in the eighth century B.C., and the society that emerged as a Graeco-Roman society from Greek and Roman imperial expansion is definitely not the Athens of Plato nor the Rome of the early Republic. Civilizational societies are not ultimate units of history but products of highly unpleasant and murderous historical processes. I do not consider it permissible to project the civilizational societies that emerge from empires and retain the differentiation of ecumenic consciousness (even if in pragmatic politics they had to restrict their ambitions) back into the societies that entered into the process.

One can speak, therefore, of the Ecumenic Age as a period in the history of mankind from which new societies emerged in which other factors than the momentum of imperial conquest became effective. When a Roman empire breaks up into a Byzantine empire, a Western Latin empire into a new expanding Islamic empire in the Near East and North Africa, there is no sense in pretending that Graeco-Roman civilization is still going on. What has arisen are new social units based on new migratory movements, cultural receptions, and expansions, which take over the form of empire created in the ecumenic period and now absorb for their justification doctrinalized spiritual outbursts as their political theologies. Ecumenic empires and their turmoil are followed by *orthodox* empires—whether in a Confucian China or a Hinduist India, in an Islamic empire, in an Eastern Greek Orthodox or a Western Latin Orthodox empire. These new imperial civilizations, which as civilizational societies are by no means identical with the societies ruled by the ecumenic empires, have lasted on the whole until the new wave of turmoil and disruption in the so-called modern period.

None of these observations on discernible structures in the history of mankind, however, must now be converted in their turn into a doctrine. Orthodox empires are exposed to disintegration when major phenomena like the Western rediscovery of pagan antiquity, and at the same time the expansion of the natural sciences, open man's consciousness to areas of reality that had been obscured by the imperially established orthodoxies. The modern period in this sense is therefore a disruption of imperial orthodoxy by a new awareness of reality. This new awareness, however, can in its turn—as it did— degenerate into an orthodoxy, this time of the progressivist ideological kind, because the new consciousness of reality has taken over from the orthodox imperial period the deformation of symbols into doctrine. The modern deformation can be characterized as an orthodoxy of alienation that excludes the most important area of reality—man's relation to the divine ground—from consciousness. This new restriction of reality, of course, will last no more than the restrictions that characterized the orthodox imperial period, because the pressure of reality cannot be resisted forever.

However, the exclusion of existential order from public consciousness, in some instances through governmental power, is not the only factor that will disintegrate contemporary ideological ascendancies. We are beset by the same problem as the founders of both the earlier ecumenic and the later orthodox empires—the fact that there is such a thing as the ethnic and cultural diversification of mankind. The empire, for instance, that we call Roman was of course not Roman. It had a core of imperial expansion in the Republic of Rome, but this republic had to transcend its own borders even in order to organize the Italian tribal societies into a confederation, and even more so when it conquered other peoples who definitely did not belong to the cultural-ethnic units of Italy, which caused their resistance. The dissolution of the Roman Empire followed roughly ethnic-cultural lines. The ethnic-cultural diversity of mankind is still an important factor in spite of the assiduous work of social and cultural destruction perpetrated by empires in the course of their expansion and self-preservation. It is unimaginable that, for instance, a Soviet empire can permanently maintain itself in its present form against the ethnic cultures of the non-Russian people who make up more than 50 percent of its population. We have similar problems on a minor scale in the United States, where the ethnic immigration that constitutes the American people has so far not been fully absorbed into a unitary civilization and where the increasing cultural self-awareness of various ethnic groups, which may take a century to become fully effective, will considerably transform American society. In the most obvious case, that of the famous Europe that does not exist, we have the problem of a considerable number of very marked and self-conscious ethnic cultures that emerged from the Christian orthodox empire in the West but have so far not yet merged into a new civilizational unit comparable to the Christian dominant establishment from which they broke out. The end of things, thus, has not come, and what a philosopher can contribute today to the understanding of an ongoing process is the understanding of the factors that make for integration and disintegration of the type just indicated.

24

Range, Constancy, Eclipse, and Equivalence
of Truth

One of the fundamental problems in every philosophy of history turned out to be the constancy of reality experienced throughout the process of compactness and transition to differentiation. The reality experienced by so-called primitives is not different from that experienced by moderns. What happens between, say, the Neolithicum and the Modern Age are the events of differentiation. The thinker who first became aware of this problem and stated its structure was Aristotle in the first two books of *Metaphysics*. He understood that his philosophical analysis of reality analyzed the same reality that was experienced by the earlier "theologizing" thinkers who expressed their experience through myth. Specifically, he refers to Hesiod and Homer. When the earlier thinkers express their experience of the origin of being through the myth of Ouranos and Gaia, they are in search of the same divine ground of being of which he himself is in search and which he recognizes as the *Nous*. The *philomythos* is to him something like a *philosophos*. In his late years he became increasingly fond of myth as a source of wisdom, since it may sometimes be more comprehensive than the structures in reality differentiated by the philosopher. He understood the relations between experiences and symbolizations on the various levels of compactness and differentiation that I have brought under the concept of *equivalence*. By equivalence is meant the recognizable identity of the reality experienced and symbolized on various levels of differentiation.

The most important consequence of this insight is the understanding of certain processes in history. When a new differentiation occurs, the area of reality newly articulated will be understood as an area of particular importance; and the over-rating of its importance amidst the joy of discovery may lead to the neglect of other areas of reality that were contained in the earlier compact experience but now are neglected. The most important such event of neglect has occurred in the modern age in the wake of the newly differentiated natural sciences. The model of the reason that is operative in the cognition of the external world has become so much the model of reason that the existentially fundamental aspects of reason in the Classic sense, as the constituent of man's humanity, were neglected and had gradually to be rediscovered in the twentieth century under the title of "existentialism," which obscures rather than clarifies the structure of reason in existence. The difficulties in this rediscovery of existential order forced Jaspers to abandon the language of existence that he favored in his earlier work and return to the language of reason (*Vernunft*) when he became aware of the derailments of existentialism, especially in the case of Sartre. This is not the only such example, however.

One of the great cases of neglect, and of eclipses of reality, occurred in the wake of Christianity. The pneumatic differentiation that we owe to Christ and Paul became, under the title of revelation, the center of Christian thought. Since revelation (the differentiation of pneumatic consciousness) had to be something entirely new, constituting an epoch in history, the presence of the pneumatic stratum in its compact form in earlier human thought was neglected and even denied. Christian doctrine assumed that man's reason is natural and, as such, a source of knowledge; in addition to this natural reason there has come into the world the new supernatural source of knowledge—revelation. That the Greek thinkers were highly conscious of having received a revelation when they discovered the *Nous* as the ground of being was simply ignored. Even today, the theophanic core of Classic philosophy is practically unknown, thanks to its eclipse by the Christian doctrine of natural reason. Hence, there is a remarkable dearth of inves-

tigations into the parallel phenomena of the Greek philosophers' and the Israelite-Christian revelation, even though the
fact that the word *prophet* is taken from the language of the
Greek poets—who knew themselves to be the prophets of the
gods in the same sense in which Israelite prophets were the
speakers (*nabi*) of the gods—should have aroused some interest.

Once the presence of revelation on various levels of compactness is recognized, one can of course develop a terminology for speaking of the parallel phenomena in adequate terms.
One can speak of theophanic events and theophanic experiences in both the noetic and the pneumatic contexts of Greek
philosophy and of Israelite and Christian revelation. And once
the parallel is recognized, one can further explore the differences between the noetic theophany of a Plato and the pneumatic theophany of a Paul. Such exploration would help considerably in understanding the structure of the philosopher's
experience, but it would also force the analyst to determine
what exactly is the content of Christian pneumatic differentiation that goes beyond the noetic differentiations of
Plato and Aristotle. This task never has been undertaken; the
problem is obscured by the language of natural reason and
revelation.

To be sure, the question is not quite outside the horizon of
Christian thinkers. A better mind like Thomas Aquinas was
very much aware of the problem. He knew that if Christ was to
be the head of all mankind, He had to be more than the head of
the members of a Christian church. Hence, Thomas formulated clearly that Christ indeed was the head of all men from
the creation of the world to its end. He was, one might say, a
true humanist who knew that Christ had come to every man,
not only to Christians, or perhaps only to theologians. Thomas' insight of course raises problems that, so far as I know, no
Christian thinker has ever dared to touch: how can Christ be
concretely the head, say, of the Babylonians or of the Greeks of
the city-state period, and how does the pneumatic presence of
His *logos* express itself in the experiences and symbolizations
of Babylonians or Egyptians? Here is a vast open field for the

philosopher of history who is seriously interested in the historical sources.

In a semiconscious way, the problem is of course present in the pursuit of studies in the fields of ancient history, the history of symbols, the history of myth, and comparative religion, because our interest in all these materials is motivated by our concern with the divine presence in these earlier symbols. Still, the historical explorers of these materials will hardly dare confess to the motive of their inquiry and state it clearly as a concern with the process of differentiation that culminates, in the Ecumenic Age, in the epochal differentiations of consciousness through philosophy, Christ, and the Apostles.

25

Consciousness, Divine Presence, and the Mystic Philosopher

A study of this critical period of the Ecumenic Age will have to face the fact that what happened is the location of the process of differentiation in the mind of man. Once consciousness or, in the Greek terminology, the *psyche* of man is understood as the site of the process, the symbolization of divine presence must shift from the intracosmic gods to the psyche of man as the site of divine presence, with the most radical expression of the experience in the Christian symbol of Incarnation.

When consciousness becomes luminous for itself as the site of divine-human cooperation in the historical process of differentiation, the end of all things has by no means come as some of the contemporaries of this great event believed. The Second Coming that would abolish the structure of this world has not happened, although it was expected by Paul and the early Christians in the near future. Instead, something entirely different happened. The symbols that expressed the experiences of the psyche, of its consciousness, of its noetic and pneumatic structure, were recognized as symbolizations of truth emerging in the process of history, which in one part is a process in this world, while in another part it is a theophanic process. Symbols at large move into the position of a secondary realization of insight; beyond this secondary insight there arises an understanding of man's tension toward the divine ground that cannot be adequately expressed by any symbolization of truth in this world. This further articulation of a stratum of experience beyond the symbolization of noetic and pneumatic divine presence is what, after Pseudo-Dionysius, came to be called mysticism. This stratum, of course, is present also before it becomes articulate in the neo-Platonically influenced Christian thinkers of the fifth century. Even Plato has a clear knowledge of relations to a divine reality that lies beyond the revelation expressed by his symbols of a Demiurge, or of the *Nous* as the third god following Kronos and Zeus in history. Mysticism, understood as the awareness of a stratum in reality that lies structurally beyond the reality of historical theophanies, even of the theophany in Christ, can be discerned in inchoate form through history as far back as we have literary records. The striking parallels between Western and Hindu mysticism, for instance, have been studied by Rudolf Otto in his *Mysticism East and West.*

Mysticism has become of considerable importance in Western history ever since the Middle Ages, when the limits of doctrinal expression of truth became visible, especially through the work of Thomas Aquinas. In the generation after Aquinas begins the split of theologizing between the nominalism of Ockham and the mysticism of Eckhart. Nominalist and mystical faith have remained ever since two important strands in Western intellectual history. The nominalism of a dogma that has separated from experience, and therefore can no longer be controlled by recourse to experience, has become the publicly dominant form of the West because it was, beginning with the eighteenth century, adopted as the intellectual form of ideologizing. In this situation, when the various doctrinal verities begin to fight one another, mysticism becomes again and again the concern of philosophers. In the sixteenth century, when there were eight religious civil wars in France, Jean Bodin recognized that the struggle between the various theological truths on the battlefield could be appeased only by understanding the secondary importance of doctrinal truth in relation to mystical insight. He wanted his sovereign, the king of France, to be, if not a mystic, at least advised by a mystic like himself in order to stand above the dogmatomachy. My careful study of the work of Bodin in the early thirties gave me my first full understanding of the function of mysticism in a time of social disorder. I still remember Bodin's *Lettre à Jan Bautru* as one of the most important documents to affect my own thought. In the twentieth century, when the dogmatomachy is no longer that of theological but of ideological sects, a similar understanding of the problem has again been reached by Henri Bergson in his *Les deux sources de la morale et de la religion.* I doubt that Bergson has the same stature as a mystic as Bodin, but these two French spiritualists are for me the representative figures for the understanding of order in times of spiritual disorder.

26

Revolution, the Open Society, and Institutions

Regarding the institutional realization of existential order, American society seems to have certain advantages over other national societies in the Western world. But I must first of all admit that in that matter I am biased because, after all, I had to run for my life from the political environment in Central Europe, and I was received with kindness in America. That of course created prejudice. Still, I hope that the following observations will not be colored too much by it.

There is first to be considered the problem of the Western revolution. Oswald Spengler observed that the revolutions that occurred before 1789—meaning the English and the American revolutions—were of a conservative type, retaining the cultural structure of Western civilization. With the French Revolution, in his opinion, begins a movement of destruction of Western culture. These formulations are somewhat abstract, but they can be elaborated by more concrete observations. Obviously a revolution like the American is distinguished from a French or Russian, or from a German National Socialist revolution, by the fact that it was able to create successfully an open society, with a minimum of violence required for its imposition. Of the major revolutions it is, one might say, the only one that has been truly successful. A good deal of animosity against America is to be found among French and German intellectuals because of this success: such a revolution should not be successful because the intellectuals want to make a revolution of their own in the tradition of the French destruction of cultural order. The animosity of the French revolutionary revolt in the name of Reason, and of a Supreme Being, against the Christian order, not too pleasantly represented in eighteenth-century France by the Church and its clergy, has no real parallel in America. We have in this country a society based on a revolutionary tradition that is not animated by the just-intimated anti-Christian animosity. However, waves of European influence also reach America; our intellectuals are strongly influenced by the European, especially the French, type of intellectualism and, more recently, by German Hegelianism and Marxism, as well as by its Russian variations.

These influences are in conflict with the American tradition. A good deal of the contemporary spiritual turmoil, the famous "divided society," is due to an absorption of the French-German type of incomplete revolution in opposition to the successful American revolution. That a large sector of American intellectuals is anti-American must be acknowledged, even if they would deny it; it is the same anti-Americanism that is to be found among European intellectuals. This anti-Americanism, setting aside certain hard-core fringe movements, however, is definitely not a serious Communism—if for no other reason than because, so far as I know, the most ardent "liberal" intellectuals, short of a few scholars, are not literate enough to read thinkers of the stature of Hegel or Marx. What we have is not a Communist, or even a Marxist, movement but a para-Marxist grotesque that always breaks down in practice because the problems envisaged by Marx lie far beyond the horizon of its understanding. Still, even in this vulgarian form the movements are a disturbing factor in society to such an extent that the language of "polarization" has become quite popular. Considering the structure of American society, I very much doubt that such a polarization has occurred. What really has happened is an inconsiderate, and partly illiterate, intellectual movement that inadvertently has polarized itself out of the American social reality and now has to pay the price of defeat for its pragmatic inadvertency.

Under one aspect this American polarization out of reality has certain similarities with the parallel European intellectual developments. The famous year 1968, with its riot in Paris, revealed if anything the nonexistence of a revolutionary situation. Raymond Aron saw quite rightly what the problem is when he gave his analysis of the events the title *La Révolution introuvable*—making himself quite unpopular by this analysis. That movements of this kind, polarizing themselves out of reality, could arise at all and create considerable public noise, was possible only because American society is beset by a number of social problems that require solutions too long delayed. There is the obvious problem of the black population and its status. Under the American historical conditions of immigration and slavery with racially and ethnically identifiable groups, the inevitable status of lower classes receives an unpleasant tinge because the lower classes are, at the same time, recognizable as ethnic or racial groups. Then there is, or rather was, the problem of the Vietnam War. Whether it was necessary in the national interest to engage in that war is very much open to question; but once it was started it had to be carried through to some sort of conclusion, because one cannot simply end a war by walking out of it. Moreover, the conditions of a war against a totalitarian power faced the American government with problems, which it had also to face in the war against Hitler, but which in the Vietnam War were aggravated by the remoteness of the events from the daily experience of the American people. The principal problem to which I refer is the fact that war against a totalitarian power, with the ruling group of totalitarian sectarians firm in its faith and willing to sacrifice the people to the bitter end for its domination, can only end with the horrors of physical destruction—that we know from the Hitler case. The same problem arose in Vietnam. The North Vietnamese government did not hesitate for a moment to have the Vietnamese people exposed to the destruction of war; and from the American side, especially through the television reports, the destruction was brought home to the American people as a destruction worked by the American army. That a war has two parties, and that the destruction was caused by the other party, who happened to be the military victim of the destruction, was simply not raised into consciousness. The bombing of German cities into vast fields of rubble, as well as the mass killings of the civilian population, as for instance in the bombardment of Hamburg where it was estimated that in one night there were more than forty thousand casualties, was taken with equanimity. Comparable destruction on a minor scale in an underdeveloped country aroused horror. That these horrors were caused by ideological sectarians and not by the American government was disregarded.

On this occasion the enormous power of the mass media under the control of the intellectual establishment became manifest. For the historian it is a fact of first importance for the understanding of certain trends in American society that it was possible to convert the military defeat of the Communists in the Tet offensive of 1968 into an American defeat through the propaganda of the mass media. Similar transformations occurred on occasion of the famous invasion of Cambodia. The fact that Cambodia had been invaded by a Communist army from North Vietnam, and that a military expedition against an invasion is not in its turn an invasion, did not deter the intellectuals from falsifying the facts into an atrocious American aggression. Similar minor transformations by the intellectuals occurred in the case of the famous bombings of the dikes in North Vietnam, or in the transformation, through deliberate lies, of the bombing of military targets in Hanoi into a carpet-bombing against the civilian population. The examples just enumerated indicate to the historian a serious problem in the intellectual sector of American society—*i.e.*, willful divorce from reality and violent aggressiveness in the pursuit of utopian dreams. Since this intellectual disease is not confined to journalists and television reporters but has penetrated deeply into the academic world, and through the academic world into the education of the younger generation, one must recognize in these trends a danger to democratic government which, after all, has to rely on contact with reality in the population at large.

Nothing lasts forever, and the present "polarization" will pass away, too. For the time being, however, the rational conduct of politics by the American government is seriously impaired because governmental action in conflict with the utopian fantasies of the moment has become practically impossible. How far this restriction of the American range of action, because of intellectuals who have lost contact with reality, will pose a danger to the country, only the future can show. Certainly we are confronted today with a massive social force of aggressive, intellectual dishonesty that penetrates the academic world, as well as other sectors of society, that will beg for correction in one form or another if the situation should ever become really critical.

27

Eschatology and Philosophy: The Practice of Dying

Once certain structures of reality become differentiated and are raised to articulate consciousness, they develop a life of their own in history. One of the important insights gained by philosophers, as well as by the prophets of Israel and by the early Christians, is the movement in reality toward a state beyond its present structure. So far as the individual human being is concerned, this movement obviously can be consummated only through his personal death. The great discovery of the Classic philosophers was that man is not a "mortal," but a being engaged in a movement toward immortality. The *athanatizein*—the activity of immortalizing—as the substance of the philosophers' existence is a central experience in both Plato and Aristotle. In the same manner, the great experience and insight of Paul was the movement of reality beyond its present structure of death into the imperishable state that will succeed it through the grace of God—*i.e.*, into the state of *aphtharsia* or imperishing. This movement toward a state of being beyond the present structure injects a further tension into existential order inasmuch as life has to be conducted in such a manner that it will lead toward the state of imperishability. Not everybody, however, is willing to attune his life to this movement. Quite a few dream of a shortcut to perfection right in this life. The dream of reality transfigured into imperishable perfection in this world, therefore, becomes a constant in history as soon as the problem has been differentiated. Already the Jewish apocalyptic thinkers expected the misery of the successive empires of which they were the victims soon to be superseded by a divine intervention that would produce the state of glory and the end of empire. Even Paul expects a Second Coming in the time of the living and revises the dream only under the impact of the experience of believers in Christ dying before the Second Coming.

Metastatic expectation of a new world succeeding the old one in the time of the presently living has become a permanent factor of disturbance in social and political reality. The movement had been suppressed by the main church with more or less success; at least the apocalyptic expectations were pushed into sectarian fringe movements. But beginning with the Reformation these fringe movements moved more and more into the center of the stage; and the replacement of Christian by secularist expectations has not changed the structure of the problem.

In the modern period, an important new factor entered the situation when the expectation of divine intervention was replaced by the demand for direct human action that will produce the new world. Marx, for instance, expected the transformation of man into superman from the blood intoxication of a violent revolution. When the expected transformation through blood intoxication did not occur in 1848, he settled for a transitional period that he called the dictatorship of the proletariat. But at least Marx still knew that external actions alone, like the appropriation of the means of industrial production by the government, did not produce the desired transformation. On the upper level of Marxist thinkers this point is still clear. The establishment of a Communist government is an external event that is supposed, in due course, to produce the expected transfiguration into superhuman perfection. Marx knew perfectly well that the establishment of a Communist government meant in itself no more than the aggravation of the evils of a capitalistic system to their highest potential. On the vulgarian level of the later Marxist sectarians, and especially of contemporary utopians, the understanding of this problem has disappeared and been replaced by something like a magic of action. The eschatological state of perfection will be reached through direct violence. The experience of a movement in reality beyond its structure has been transformed into the magic vulgarity of aggressive destruction of social order.

Still, though this experience is exposed to the vulgarian transformations just indicated, the experience is real. Otherwise it could not have this permanently motivating effect that is visible even in the deformations. Hence, every philosophy of history must take cognizance of the fact that the process of history is not immanent but moves in the In-Between of this-worldly and other-worldly reality. Moreover, this In-Between character of the process is experienced, not as a structure in infinite time, but as a movement that will eschatologically end in a state beyond the In-Between and beyond time. No philosophy of history can be considered to be seriously dealing with the problems of history unless it acknowledges the fundamental eschatological character of the process.

The understanding of the eschatological movement requires a revision of the deformations that the concepts of Classic philosophy have suffered at the hands of interpreters who want the nature of man to be a fixed entity. The Classic philosophers were quite aware of the problems of eschatology, as I have just indicated. They knew that they were engaged in the practice of dying, and that the practice of dying meant the practice of immortalizing. The expansion of this experience into an understanding of history makes it, of course, impossible to erect concepts like the nature of man into constants in reality. This, however—and there lies the difficulty of understanding the problem—does *not* mean that the nature of man can be transfigured within history. In the process of history, man's nature does no more than become luminous for its eschatological destiny. The process of its becoming luminous, however, though it adds to the understanding of human nature and its problems, does not transmute human nature in the here-and-now of spatio-temporal existence. The consciousness of the eschatological expectation is an ordering factor in existence; and it makes possible the understanding of man's existence as that of the *viator* in the Christian sense—the wanderer, the pilgrim toward eschatological perfection—but this pilgrimage still is a pilgrim's progress in this world.

This eschatological tension of man's humanity, in its dimensions of person, society, and history, is more than a matter of theoretical insight for the philosopher; it is a practical question. As I have said, Plato and Aristotle were very much aware that the action of philosophizing is a process of immortalizing in this world. This action does not come to its end with Plato and Aristotle; it continues, though in every concrete situation the philosopher has to cope with the problems he encounters in his own position concretely. If the Classic philosophers had to cope with the difficulties created by a dying myth and an active Sophistic aggressiveness, the philosopher in the twentieth century has to struggle with the "climate of opinion," as Whitehead called this phenomenon. Moreover, in his concrete work he has to absorb the enormous advances of the sciences, both natural and historical, and to relate them to the understanding of existence. That is a considerable labor, considering the mountains of historical materials that have become known in our time.

A new picture of history is developing. The conceptual penetration of the sources is the task of the philosopher today; the results of his analysis must be communicated to the general public and, if he happens to be a professor in a university, to the students. These chores—of keeping up with the problems, of analyzing the sources, and of communicating the results—are concrete actions through which the philosopher participates in the eschatological movement of history and conforms to the Platonic-Aristotelian practice of dying.